AMERICAN
WOODWORKER

USEFUL TECHNIQUES
for
WOODCARVERS

The best from **WOODCARVING** *magazine*

USEFUL TECHNIQUES
for
WOODCARVERS

The best from **WOODCarving** *magazine*

GUILD OF MASTER CRAFTSMAN PUBLICATIONS LTD

This collection first published 1998
by Guild of Master Craftsman Publications Ltd,
Castle Place, 166 High Street, Lewes, East Sussex BN7 1XU

© GMC Publications 1998

ISBN 1 86108 079 4

Printed and bound by Kyodo Printing (Singapore) under the supervision of
MRM Graphics, Winslow, Buckinghamshire, UK

Front and back cover photographs supplied by Ted Vincent

CONTENTS

NOTES

Please note that names, addresses, prices etc. were correct at the time the articles were originally published, but may since have changed.

INTRODUCTION

When people take up woodcarving for the first time, or when they seek to improve on basic skills, they are always hungry for technical information on the 'how-to' of the craft, whether using hand tools or modern, labour-saving machines.

They want to know how to master their wood and tools, both for the pleasure of using them skilfully, and the satisfaction of producing a good work.

As Editor of *Woodcarving* magazine, I have sought to demystify the craft, and to satisfy that hunger for technical advice, with detailed, practical instruction from some of the best craftsmen around the world.

In this book of articles selected from *Woodcarving* magazine, you will find countless hints and tips from experienced woodcarvers, both amateur and professional, who willingly share their expertise.

Here are skilled craftsmen who use both traditional hand tools and modern power equipment to achieve stunning results, and who will encourage you to emulate their success.

Some authors, like Dick Onians, who has been writing for the magazine since the very first issue, concentrate on the more traditional aspects of carving technique, while newer writers, such as Ted Vincent, will stretch your imagination with more experimental ideas.

Whatever your level of commitment and skill, I am confident you will find material within these pages to both instruct and inspire you to develop your interest in and expertise at carving wood.

Nick Hough
Editor
Woodcarving

EARTHWORKS

THE COMPLEX RELATIONSHIP BETWEEN NATURAL AND MAN-MADE LANDSCAPES PROVIDED TED VINCENT'S INSPIRATION FOR AN EXHIBITION.

These four pieces were done specifically for my exhibition at Chichester District Museum earlier this year. As with previous works, they drew their inspiration from the Rother Valley.

POND LIFE

Within the theme of *Diatoms* I was searching for a form to express the idea of growth. After considering various possibilities, I became interested in using these beautiful, single-celled, microscopic water plants, which are invisible to the naked eye.

Magnified drawings in *The Observer Book of Pond Life* showed them as attractive forms. I thought their decorative shapes and sculpted surfaces with fine lines and textures would present many possibilities for carving.

I selected a number of diatoms of varying shape and complexity, produced a series of drawings on tracing paper, and juggled these around to form a composition.

After exploring various ways of setting the diatoms out in patterns along a 600mm, 2ft stream of water, I decided it would make a stronger image if I made a complex arrangement of shape and form at one end, and led the eye to this along the perspective of the stream.

The stream itself was made by cutting the wood to shape on the bandsaw and by working the surface with a gouge to represent water, making the marks diminish in size as they reached the point.

I made the curved shape as thin as possible to give a very lightweight and visually simple form that provided a background to the more dynamic and complex shape of the diatoms.

Some of the diatoms were carved from the same piece of wood. Others, like the trumpet-shaped, floral motif at the top of the design, were carved separately and glued into place as the composition evolved.

The piece grew as it went along, suggesting to me ways to develop the

Top left **Microscopic water plants are represented as part of a flowing stream.**

Centre left **The sculpture presents many different diatoms as a collage.**

Left **Detail was carved with small gouges and chisels.**

asymmetrical pattern I was looking for. Some shapes were exclusively carved using gouges and small chisels to create various texture and surface details. On some shapes I used a fretsaw to cut lines through the forms, which were then carved in to create a full three dimensional image.

The diagrams I was working from, although fairly detailed, were all 2-D images and gave no account of the depth, so I interpreted thickness in a way that made the composition grow out from the background.

Once I had set out the overall design I completed the carving using small gouges and a variety of burrs and dentist drills in a flexible drive tool to incise and remove deep undercuts in the design.

Because of the level of detail it was important to use good quality lime (*Tilia Vulgaris*) and vital to keep all carving tools sharp and polished throughout the operation.

I have always felt carving was very much part of the decorative tradition, and see this method of working as a way of developing this area in a modern idiom.

FOSSIL FORMS

Buried Fossils was a development in a series of simplified landscape pieces which were distinct from the combined carved and constructed pieces I also produce. As with other pieces of work of this kind, the composition was not specifically pre-planned, just a notion about an undulating surface with fossil forms trapped in the landscape.

I began with a piece of lime 305 x 305 x 50mm, 12 x 12 x 2in. I made no drawing or sketch to begin with but worked initially from the feeling I had developed from a visit to a particular piece of downland.

Using a 25mm, 1in gouge, I established the contour of the hills, which set out the basis of the composition.

When I began to place the fossils in the composition, I used the British

Above **Fossil forms trapped in the landscape.** Right **Hollowing out. A difficult process in this case.**

....

Museum (Natural History) publication *British Mesozoic Fossils* as reference.

Both forms were based on echinoids which conform to a circular pattern, so I drew directly onto the wood with a compass, marking a series of circles radiating out from the centre of each, and used these as guide marks to carve the basic form.

I used a small flat chisel to establish the semi-spherical forms of the echinoid. I finished the surface with scrapers and steel wool to give a well finished form into which I could carve the detail.

I marked out the divisions that made the surface pattern and the holes in the centre in pencil, and this cut into the surface, following the pencil line with a very sharp, thin scalpel blade so as to not break out.

Then, using a small, flat chisel, I removed sections of the wood to give a very low relief. I wanted to keep the detail as subtle as possible and removed only about 1.5mm, 1/16in. Any blemishes were removed by scraping.

The decorative holes in the centre of each fossil were achieved by first drilling a pilot hole of 13mm, 1/2in, then carving away the insides of the fossils from behind with a gouge.

I had to be careful at this point, as

the wood where I had carved from the inside of the form was very thin, to give the feeling of the delicacy of the fossil against the robust nature of the surrounding landscape.

This was an important part of the composition as I intended to exhibit the finished work on a hollow plinth, so spectators would look into deep blackness through the holes. The void formed a strong part of the design.

I paid attention to making the shape of the holes exact, achieving a crisp edge with knife and needle files. The surrounding landscape was carved with various sized gouges, finishing to a smooth, continuous surface with scrapers.

I find a cabinet scraper is a versatile tool which, unlike sandpaper, does not clog the grain so you can achieve a very clean surface. I finished the surface with two coats of sanding sealer rubbed down between each application with 0000 wire wool.

As well as looking at my work, people like to touch it, and the tactile quality of this piece was just as important as its visual appeal.

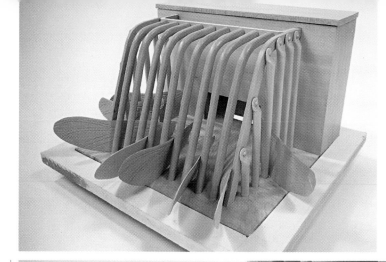

DRAGONFLY WINGS

This piece combined a variety of techniques of carving, shaping and fabricating, and was made from lime taken from the same plank of timber to ensure evenness of colour and surface. I developed the idea from observing a sluice gate where various fragments floating on the water had become caught in the bars.

As this was a fairly complex structure, I first made a maquette in cardboard. Although this gave only an overall idea, it saved a lot of time and costly material. I can develop an idea so far using drawing, but I find the hands-on experience of the model gives a full and informed picture of the idea.

Once I had decided on a set of dimensions, I began the job by making the bars of the cage. Using the bandsaw I cut a set of blanks, which I sanded to a round cross-section, keeping a close eye on the shape, particularly at the bend.

I took them to their final dimension with a curved scraper. It was important they were accurate and of the same diameter, as they all had to fit into the same size holes in the base.

The next stage was to make the water base. This first had to be cut to shape to fit with the wall to which the cage was connected. Once the holes had been drilled to accept the bars, I carved the pattern of the water, giving the impression of it rushing towards the sluice and tumbling down through it. The box representing the wall was a simple structure with holes cut to receive the cage.

Having made most of the components I came to the more delicate and detailed work of the dragonfly wings. I made some card templates, traced from drawings I had done of the wings of a dead dragonfly, and used these to mark out the eight separate wings.

I cut them from a fairly thick, 25mm, 1in piece of lime, which allowed me to sculpt each one with a

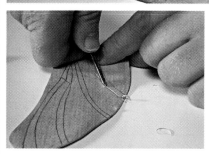

Top **Dragonfly wings, inspired by detritus stuck in a drainage grille.**
Centre **The wings give the impression of being held against the grille by water pressure.**
Above left **Carving the wings.**
Above right **Building the grille.**

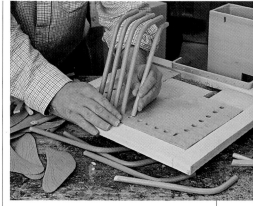

twist in it, giving a greater feeling of three dimensions than if they were flat. I shaped them on a drum sander attached to a De Walt radial arm saw, finishing them as thin as possible with a curved cabinet scraper.

Once I had arrived at the right curvature and thickness, I marked out the pattern of the ribs on both sides of each wing using tracing paper. I first

followed the pencil line with a scalpel, being careful not to cut too deeply as the wings were very thin and I was cutting on both sides.

Then, using a 1mm, $\frac{1}{32}$in gouge and the scalpel line as a guide, I cut lines to represent the pattern of the wings. I did all eight wings in succession, keeping the gouge very sharp throughout, to ensure a crisp cut and flowing line. This gave a complex organic rhythm that played an important part in the composition, providing contrast to the regular, severe pattern of the bars of the cage.

Having assembled all the components, I gave everything two coats of sanding sealer, rubbed down with wire wool, and assembled and glued together all the parts.

I placed the wings trapped between the bars to give the feeling they were being forced by the pressure of the water towards the weir.

Below left **Water pouring through a hole in a wall.**
Above left **The wood was cut right through at the bottom of the fall.**
Above right **Fitting the waterfall.**

....

MOVEMENT

As with the *Dragonfly Wings*, I had a specific idea of the image I was after for *Waterfall*: water falling from a hole in a wall. The focus was very much on the water and the form it made as it gushed out. I took lots of photographs of my subject at various shutter speeds, capturing the movement and frozen effect of the water.

To create the water, I began with a large piece of lime 760 x 150 x 150mm, 30 x 6 x 6in. This was a clean and well seasoned piece purchased

from W. L. West's of Petworth, who provide very good quality English lime.

I first removed the concave shape that would form the back of the waterfall, initially using a large gouge and mallet.

Having created what I regarded as a satisfactory shape, I turned my attention to the front, following the curvature set by what I had removed from the back to a basic shape. Again using a large gouge, I carved the front of the waterfall, then working from the top downwards, using first a 13mm, ½in gouge, I created an overall pattern.

Next, using two small gouges I cut marks to represent the flow of the falling water, piercing through the thin wood as it got nearer to the ground to represent the water breaking up. I then worked the back in the same manner.

I wanted to present the water in a particular way, isolated, not quite touching the ground at the bottom, and flowing from nowhere at the top. To achieve this effect, I built a neutral box which was painted white and, in effect, formed the plinth out of which the water flowed.

The front and a small part of the back were made from lime with a brick pattern incised into it. Not only did it represent a material but it also gave a clear idea of scale.

The square hole the water flowed from became a focus in the design, and I carved a stream to run through the plinth, giving the feeling to the spectator of an underground spring that fed the waterfall. ●

De Walt (Elu Power Tools)
210 Bath Road, Slough,
Berkshire SL1 3YD
Tel: 01753 576717

W.L. West & Son Ltd (timber merchants), Selham, Petworth, West Sussex GU28 0PJ
Tel: 01798 861611

Second hand tools from Leeside Tool Shop, Burntell Road, Yapton, West Sussex BN18 0HP
Tel: 01243 554056

Ted Vincent is a senior lecturer in the School of Three-dimensional Design at Kingston University, Surrey. He is happy to advise anyone entering an education in 3-D design. His exhibitions, sponsored by the Environment Agency, John Blake Hydraulic Engineers and Canon UK, are held at Chichester District Museum. Tel: 01243 784683.

BODY BUILDING

IN THE FIRST OF TWO ARTICLES ON SCULPTING THE HUMAN TORSO, DICK ONIANS BEGINS WITH A STUDY OF ANATOMY

The idea of sculpting the human torso without head and limbs would probably not have occurred to man if he had not been attracted by the wreckage of ancient civilisations such as Greece and Rome.

The torso is the most solid and compact part of the body and therefore most likely to endure intact.

Seventh Century BC Greek figures look like modern wood sculptures where front and side profiles are cut out with a bandsaw and the corners rounded.

But in 300 years the Greeks shook off the rigidity of their first attempts and produced lifelike figures.

Their aim was a god-like perfection, and mathematical proportions were seen as divine. The result was, as each carver tried to make his sculptures more alive than his master's

he also made the forms as close to the ideal as possible.

It is also easier to plan a sculpture if there are set proportions for the parts of the body.

With the Greek example in mind, carvers wishing to represent the human form should try to improve upon, rather than copy poor sculptures.

The best way to start is to make a thorough study of the figure by life drawing or modelling. An excellent aid to this is anatomical study.

This helps to show how the various lumps and hollows are formed, which parts can change shape and which are hard and soft.

Though fat, fascia tissue and skin soften the details of bones and muscles, they cannot hide them altogether, nor can clothes.

SKELETON

Carvers of the human figure should know the basic skeleton and the main muscles visible at the surface. They should then be able to avoid making square, disjointed and impossibly contorted figures.

A good way to start is with modelling the torso, since the armature is uncomplicated and there are no arms to get in the way of the ribcage and its muscles.

True modelling involves building up from the inside, not carving excess clay from a block.

When modelling a torso you do not usually work from so far in as I do here, but it is worth doing once to learn why the surface is as it is.

The spinal column or spine keeps the shoulders apart from the pelvis so we start with that. It is made up of 33 or 34 *vertebrae*, with *inter-vertebral discs* between those above the pelvis.

The bumps which you can feel down the middle of your back are long *processes* which grow backwards from

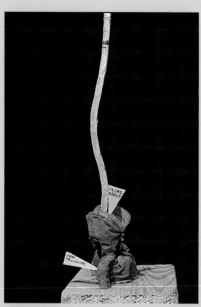

The armature of the spine made from square aluminium wire. Note the curvature of the side view with the pelvis sketched in clay, showing the iliac crest sloping down to the anterior superior spine at the front.

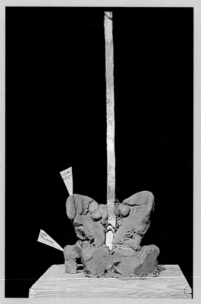

The spine and pelvis, front view. the iliac crest is held on a wire armature. Note the relationship between the iliac crest and the great trochanter and the position of the anterior superior spine.

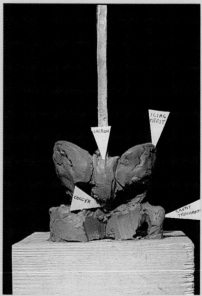

Back view of the pelvis showing the sacrum between the halves of the pelvis.

every *vertebra*. They are known as spines, which can be confusing.

The spinal column seen from front or back is a straight line, but seen sideways is gently S shaped. At its base in the small of the back or lumbar region it curves backwards.

Five *vertebrae* are here fused together to form the *sacrum* which continues the same curve tapering into the *coccyx*, which curves forwards again.

Above the lumbar region the spine curves backwards as it ascends and then forwards from near the top of the ribcage or thorax.

It returns more or less to the vertical at the top of the neck where it fits under the middle of the skull. Seen from behind, the *sacrum* is roughly triangular and links the two halves of the pelvis.

PELVIS

The pelvis forms half a cup to hold the intestines and other organs. But the parts that interest the sculptor most are the outer rim or *iliac crest* that runs from the *sacrum* up, around and down at the front to the *anterior superior spine* at each side, the bony lump just in from the side of the body below the waist, the *symphysis pubis*, the lump which we do not see because it is behind the genitals but to which are fastened some of the *adductor* muscles that we use to pull the legs together, and the hip socket (*acetabulum*) in which the top of the thigh bone, the *femur*, sits.

The *acetabulum* is also invisible because the ball on the head of the femur is on the end of a short stalk almost at right angles to the main shaft of the bone.

On the outer side of the bone at the top is a big lump called the *great trochanter*. Lumps (or *processes*), ridges, spines and plates of bone are where strong muscles are attached.

The pelvis is composed of large plates with thick rims and, being in the middle of the body, has numerous powerful muscles attached.

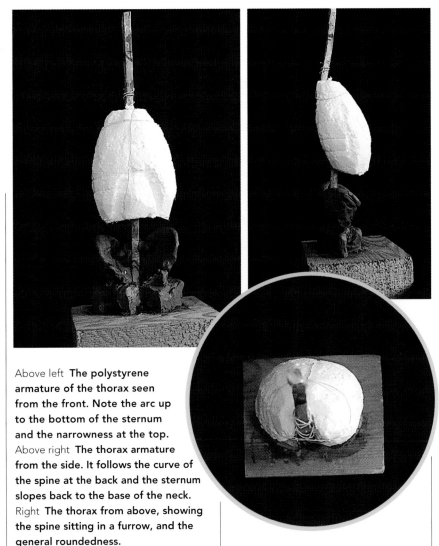

Above left **The polystyrene armature of the thorax seen from the front. Note the arc up to the bottom of the sternum and the narrowness at the top.**
Above right **The thorax armature from the side. It follows the curve of the spine at the back and the sternum slopes back to the base of the neck.**
Right **The thorax from above, showing the spine sitting in a furrow, and the general roundedness.**

The gap between the highest part of the *iliac crest* and the lowest rib is about a finger's thickness. It is possible to build the thorax rib by rib, but it is safe to regard it as basically egg-shaped, with the little end at the top, and the bottom end cut off.

The ribs curve in towards the spine and appear to form a valley down the back with the row of *vertebral spines* standing out in the middle.

If the back is well muscled these spines barely project unless the back is bent forwards. The two bottom ribs at each side float in front.

Above them the ribs are linked at the front by cartilage which arches up to the *solar plexus* which is at the bottom end of the *sternum*.

The *sternum* is a jointed bone that runs from this point to the top of the thorax. From the front it appears dagger-shaped, but viewed sideways it curves and slopes backwards to the neck.

The top five ribs are joined to it by more or less horizontal strips of cartilage, which flattens out the middle area.

THORAX

On my model I made the thorax out of expanded polystyrene as it is light, easily shaped and, when anchored with wire to the spinal column, stops the clay from sliding down. I was also able to push some wire through it to support the tops of the arms.

The arms are easily moved in many directions because they are joined to the thorax only by muscles and where the collarbones (*clavicles*) rest at each side of the top of the *sternum*.

The shoulder blades (*scapulae*) are attached to the back by muscles. They are roughly triangular plates, curved to fit the thorax.

Near the top, which is the short side of the *scapula*, there is a ridge (spine) that slopes across to the outside corner and projects beyond, forming the *acromion process* which the *clavicle* rests on.

At the front there is a similar projection, the *coracoid process*. The head of the upper arm bone, the *humerus*, sits in a socket on the corner of the *scapula* below and between these two.

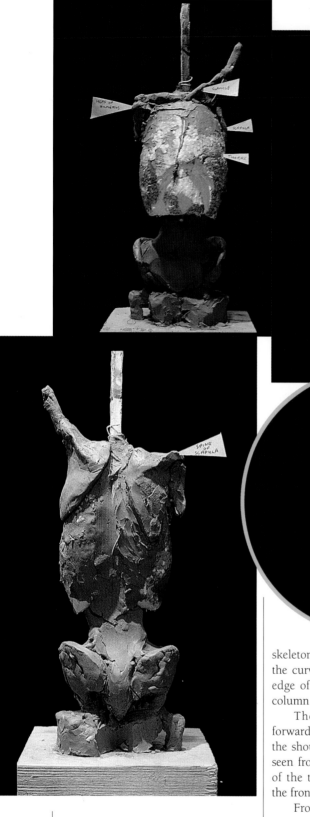

Top far left **The thorax with clavicles, showing how their angles change as the arms change position.**
Left **The side view of the thorax with clavicle, scapula and top of humerus.**
Below far left **Back view of thorax with scapulae. Note the left scapula's position. Its spine is at a steep angle and the bottom corner swings around to the side. The clay above the pelvis is simply a core.**
Left **Top view of the shoulder girdle showing the way the clavicles are S shaped, following the curve of the thorax and swinging forward to the shoulder joints. The spines of the scapulae also slope forward to the shoulders.**

them and concentrate on the superficial muscles.

They contract, harden and change shape when they are used. By adopting various postures and pushing and pulling you can feel what most of them do.

I start at the bottom with the *gluteus maximus*, the big muscle that we sit upon. It is the body's strongest muscle, used in making the body erect and in bending the thighs.

It attaches to the back of the *iliac crest* and emphasises the triangular area at the top of the cleft of the buttocks caused by the *sacrum*.

It slopes diagonally forwards and outwards from the back of the *iliac crest*, joining the rear part of the *ilio-tibial* band behind the *great trochanter*.

Seen from the side this band of fascia tissue is Y-shaped. It runs tapering down the outside of the thigh and is attached to the top of the shin bone at the knee.

The *great trochanter* sits in the angle of the Y. The front arm of the Y is joined to the *tensor fasciae latae* which continues up to the *anterior superior spine* of the pelvis.

You should be able to feel the *clavicle* and the *processes* when the arm hangs naturally. You can also feel the *great tuberosity* which sticks out on the side of the *humerus* opposite the joint and lower than the *acromion process*.

TOP VIEW
The most important view of a sculpture is from above. If you look at the skeleton from above you can see how the curvature of the thorax makes the edge of the *scapula* nearest the spinal column project.

The result is there is a slope forwards from there to the arm when the shoulders are relaxed. The *clavicles* seen from above curve around the top of the thorax, then swing forward to the front of the *acromion processes*.

From the front the *clavicles* present a virtually straight line unless the arms are raised.

On my model I have raised the left arm to show how the *clavicle* and the *scapula* move and the muscles change when the arm stretches upwards.

There are interior muscles and organs that affect the surface form, but I assume you know the general shape of the body well enough for me to miss

MUSCLES

The *gluteus medius* is a fan-shaped muscle which springs from the *iliac crest* between the other two muscles with its point on the *great trochanter*.

Because there is usually some fat on the hips and buttocks, the grooves between these three muscles are softened, but the *great trochanter* either stands out or sits in a hollow, depending on fat and posture.

Also attached to the *anterior superior spine* is a long thin muscle, the *sartorius*, which seen from the front runs diagonally across the thigh to the inside of the knee.

Between the *sartorius* and the *tensor fasciae latae* is the *rectus femoris*. The *sartorius* creates a groove between this and the group of *adductor* muscles, which form the inside of the thigh.

The main muscles of the back are the *latissimus dorsi* and the *trapezius*.

The *latissimus dorsi*, literally 'the widest of the back', is attached to the lower half of the spine, including the *sacrum*, and the back of the *iliac crest*.

It swings upwards and outwards, crossing the bottom corner of the *scapula* and twisting up into the armpit to attach to the front of the top of the *humerus*.

You can feel and see it when you raise your arm. From behind it makes the back seem to taper from the armpits to the waist.

The *trapezius* is a huge kite-shaped muscle with its bottom point in the middle of the back overlapping the two *lattissimus dorsi* muscles.

It forms a V shape up to the inner ends of the spines of the *scapulae*, runs along the tops of these spines to the meeting with the *clavicles*, then up to the base of the skull and down to the clavicles at the front.

It is the muscle that makes the shoulders slope up to the neck and makes the base of the neck wider at the back.

Attached to the underside of the outer third of the *clavicle*, to the *acromion* and to the underside of the spine of the *scapula* is the *deltoid*.

This attachment is like the base line of the triangle, the apex of which is almost halfway down the *humerus*.

Slotting up under the *deltoid* at the back is the *triceps* muscle which runs down the back of the upper arm.

The muscles of the side and front consist mainly of the breast (*pectoral*) muscles, the *external oblique* muscles and the *rectus abdominis*.

RIBCAGE

The *pectoral* muscle is a large plate-like muscle which is attached to the inner part of the *clavicle*, the *sternum* and the cartilage below. Its head twists to a point which is inserted under the *deltoid* onto the *humerus*.

If you push your fingers up between it and the *latissimus dorsi* you can feel the ribcage sloping up to the base of the neck. The nipple sits on this muscle near its lower outer edge.

Emerging from under the front edge of the *latissimus dorsi* and sloping

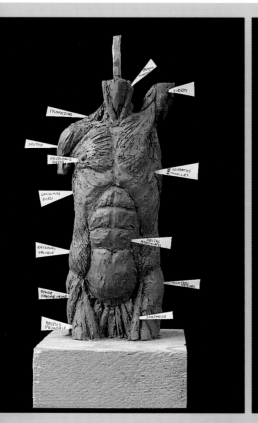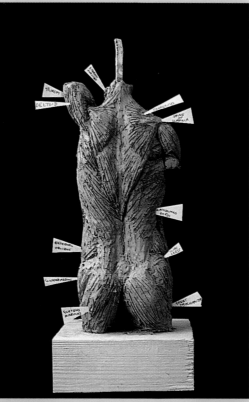

Far left **Front view of the torso without skin, fascias and fat.** Left **Back view in the same state. Note how the left scapula shows through the muscles and pushes out the latissimus dorsi at the side.**

Right **Three quarters view of left front showing the armpit and the adductor muscles on the inside of the thigh. Note the deep hollow between the pectoral and latissimus dorsi muscles that forms the armpit.**

Far right **View of the right side. Note the small bump formed by the great trochanter in the hollow below the gluteus medius with the gluteus maximus behind and the tensor fasciae latae at the front. The Y formed by the ilio-tibial band and the last two muscles contributes to the hollow.**

Below **The genitals in place in front of the symphysis pubis and the adductor muscles.**

downwards to the front of the thorax is a row of fingerlike heads to a muscle called the *serratus magnus*.

They form a zigzag groove where they slot into the *external oblique*, a tall muscle that is attached at the bottom to the *iliac crest* and at the top to the lower eight ribs.

It particularly swells out above the *iliac crest*. It is joined to its pair by a large flattened tendon or *aponeurosis* which completely covers the *rectus abdominis* from top to bottom.

At its bottom edge it joins the *Poupart's ligament* which runs from the *anterior superior iliac spine* to the *symphysis pubis*, immediately behind the genitals.

This ligament forms the curved furrow between the abdomen and the thigh. The *rectus abdominis* is an oblong muscle running from the arch at the bottom of the thorax down to *Poupart's ligament*.

When well developed it presents a great column with a groove down the middle to the waist with three horizontal grooves, the lowest of which crosses just above the navel.

At the top of the *sternum* the windpipe runs up in front of the spine surrounded by the *thyroid* and the *thyroid cartilage*. From the side this makes the front of the neck slope up and forwards repro-

ducing the slope at the back.

However, at the front the two *sterno-cleido-mastoid* muscles come down from the *mastoid processes* on the skull just behind the ears to the top of the *sternum*.

From each one another head swings out near the bottom to join the *clavicle*. This means where the *trapezius* is tapering out to the shoulders the front of the neck tapers in the opposite way.

The female torso differs from the male mainly in having breasts, a wider pelvis and different fat distribution. ●
In my next article, on page 14, I describe how I carve a torso in wood, bearing in mind the bones and muscles.

Dick Onians is senior carving tutor at the City and Guilds of London Art School. Since 1968, as well as teaching, he has been working as a professional sculptor in wood and stone. He inaugurated the City and Guilds Institute Creative Studies course in woodcarving. He also teaches a part-time woodcarving course at Missenden Abbey Adult Residential College in Buckinghamshire. His book, *Essential Woodcarving Techniques*, is published by GMC Publications.

VASED IMPROVEMENT

RATHER THAN LET A BAD BACK PUT AN END TO HIS INTRICATE CARVED VASES, MICHAEL KORHUN DESIGNED AND BUILT AN ADJUSTABLE WORK TABLE

Above **A selection of carved vases.**
Below **Already turned to shape, the vase is scribed with a compass prior to carving.**

When carving I rarely use a knife. I do all my carvings with chisels and gouges which I have designed for each specific job. They are made of tool steel, either old knives and saw blades filed down, or something as simple as the grooved spokes of an old umbrella.

My chisels are short, with the handles not more than 200mm, 8in. long. The blades range from 25 to 70mm, 1 to 2¾ inches in length. The width of the chisels can be anywhere from 5 to 13mm, ³⁄₁₆ to ½in. The skew angles of these chisels can range from 45° and 60° to 90°, and from 1.5 to 20mm, ¹⁄₁₆ to ¾in in size.

This wide variety of chisels enables me to create designs of various degrees of complexity, each one unique. In all I own approximately 200 tools, including 15 knives.

CONTROL

In carving I prefer to work with shorter chisels because they allow me greater control and stability. I not only push the tools with my hands but also my shoulders which gives me greater control of the chisel.

After completely covering a turned vase with a coat of polyurethane and wax, I place it back on the lathe to carve circumferential lines. Steadily, I place a 5mm, ³⁄₁₆in chisel on a rest leaning toward the vase.

I carefully turn the vase with one hand using the other hand to guide the chisel applied against the vase to draw the preliminary lines.

On completion of the horizontal lines on the vase I remove it from the lathe and place it vertically in a workholder. This allows me to turn the vase, so I can divide its area with a compass, vertically, depending on its size, into four, six, or eight evenly spaced sections, and from there I begin to create a design.

PATTERNS

I never plan any preliminary designs, and a lot of the time I have no idea how the final pattern will look, though certain elements will be fixed when I'm doing the initial turning.

It is important to divide the vase into equal and precise sections because problems may otherwise occur as you proceed with the work.

Above **Symmetry is all important at this stage.**

When I have sectioned off the vase I begin to chip carve out the design. As I carve notches, edges, angles, curves, squares, lines and so forth, I make sure all the angles and ends meet correctly and accurately.

With an angular chisel, I begin the notched, jagged, or tooth-like design of

The finished object, in mahogany (*Swietenia macrophylla*), padauk (*Pterocarpus spp*), poplar (*Liriodendron tulipifera*) and ebony (*Diospyrus spp*) 430 x 305mm, 17 x 12in.

Cutting and parts

Table	Qty	
top (26 x 18in)	1	25¼ x 17¼ x ¾in
top frame	2	26 x 3 ½ x ¾in
	2	18 x 3½ x ¾in
base (20 x 13¼in)	1	19¼ x 12½ x ¾in
base frame	2	18 x 3½ x ¾in
	2	13¼ x 2½ x ¾in
lifters	8	2¼ x ¾ x 24in
side bars	2	2 x 2 x 13in
inside slide		
aluminium angle	1	6 x 2 x 2 x ¼in
slider	1	17 x 8 x ¾in
slider rails	2	13 x 1 x ¹³⁄₁₆in
back plate	1	13 x 10 x ¾in
front plate	1	10 x 7 x ¾in
feet	2	6 x 4 x ¾in
winder	1	¾ x 12in diameter
	1	¾ x 4in diameter
worktop	1	28 x 26 x ½in
sides	2	26 x 3in
sill	1	28 x 3in
ratchet	1	20 x 2 x 2in cut at 1in intervals.
stand	2	18 x 2 x 2in
Parts		
table	4	⅜in bolts, 2½in long
	6	⅜in bolts, 1½in long
	4	⅜in machine bolts 2½in long
slider	12	no.10, 1½in wood screws
	3	no.10, 1¼in wood screws
winder screw	1	30 x ¾in

a repeat pattern and proceed to the end. I have to keep in mind how much space I have remaining.

I slightly increase or decrease the size of the teeth in the design to create the appearance of uniformity. I have to avoid having space for only half a tooth at the end of the pattern.

Working on a piece covered with a finish can be extremely difficult as it does not allow for mistakes. If a mistake is made it is obvious and is quite difficult to correct as the finish is broken. I experimented with many variations before I settled upon this system.

The outside coat on the vase, finished in a dark-coloured stain, creates a contrast to the carvings on the wood. The carvings give the impression of inlaid work rather than carving.

I buff the carved area with a stiff brush to eliminate all unwanted fragments, wood, dust, and small particles that might be caught in the corners.

POSTURE

With my injured back I find it difficult to work in a stooped position. I do most of the work sitting down, but carving in the sitting position also poses a problem for me because each piece I work on is a different size and height.

It is feasible to carve plates of varied diameters on a table top in the sitting position. However, carving a tall vase poses problems.

I looked at commercially available stands but none were exactly what I was looking for, so I built a table to my own specifications.

I can lower it to a height of

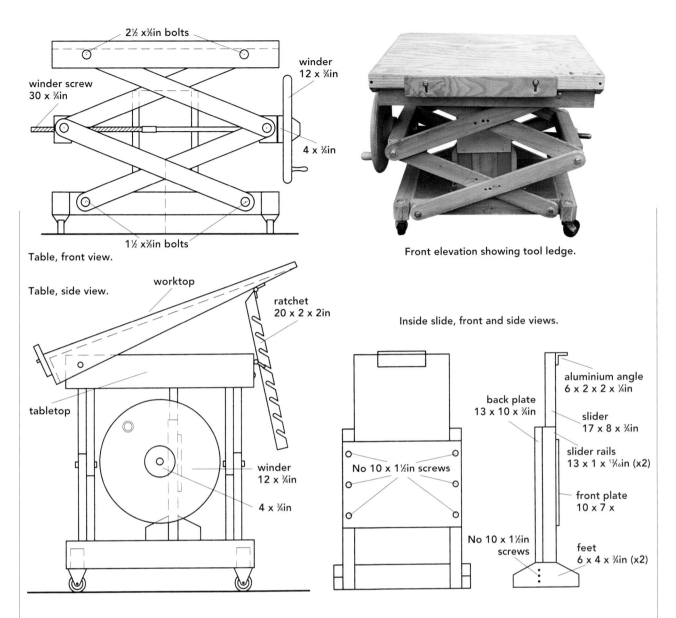

2½ x ⅜in bolts

winder screw
30 x ¾in

winder
12 x ¾in

4 x ¾in

1½ x ⅜in bolts

Table, front view.

Front elevation showing tool ledge.

Table, side view.

worktop

ratchet
20 x 2 x 2in

tabletop

winder
12 x ¾in

4 x ¾in

Inside slide, front and side views.

back plate
13 x 10 x ¾in

No 10 x 1½in screws

No 10 x 1½in
screws

aluminium angle
6 x 2 x 2 x ¼in

slider
17 x 8 x ¾in

slider rails
13 x 1 x ¹³⁄₁₆in (x2)

front plate
10 x 7 x

feet
6 x 4 x ¾in (x2)

Side elevation showing winder.

Rear elevation showing angle and height adjusters.

432mm, 17in or raise it to a height of 815mm, 32in depending on the subject to be carved.

This table, incorporating criss-crossed legs fastened together with a centre screw, allows me to set the table top at any desired height, and to carve

in comfort.

It also makes the whole process easier, especially on cross-wise designs.

The chair I sit in also adjusts to various heights. A pair of locking castors allows for full mobility or firm immobility as required. ●

Michael Korhun was born in Jazyny in the central Poltava region of the Ukraine in 1924. His family were farmers, but his father was a craftsman who made violins. After the war, when he was a prisoner in a work camp, he studied sculptural carving with Russian carver Arkadi Lapsenkov. In 1952 he moved to Troy, New York, USA, where he still lives, and worked as a toolmaker.

BODYWORK

IN HIS FINAL ARTICLE ON SCULPTING A HUMAN TORSO, DICK ONIANS COMPLETES THE CARVING IN WOOD

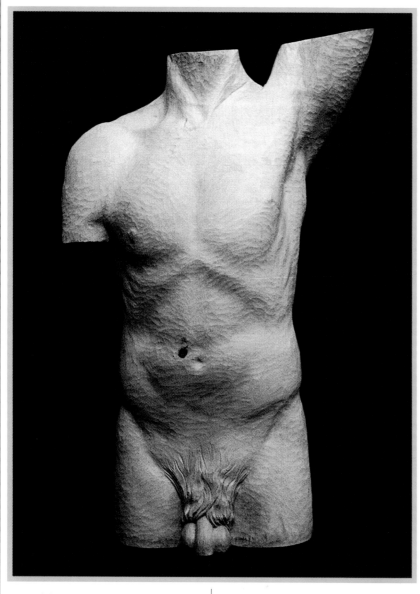

One of the most pathetic objects I have seen, yet one of the most instructive, was a plaster cast of the torso of a girl who had drowned in the Seine during the 1890s. There must have been a time when all art schools had a copy.

What struck me most was the flatness of the forms. From a distance

Finished carving from the front. Note sterno-cleido-mastoid muscles forming a V around the windpipe, not quite symmetrical because of the raised arm. The right clavicle is visible with hollows above and below. The left clavicle is mostly lost behind the pectoral. Note the rhythms formed by shadows.

they could not be read, but all merged together without defining shadows.

When Rodin submitted his *Age Of Bronze* sculpture of a male nude to the Paris Salon it looked so lifelike he was accused of taking a mould from a real person.

Eventually the jurors were convinced he was right as, like all good sculptors, he had omitted some details and exaggerated essential forms to create the shadows needed to make it readable.

In modern art schools this skill is seldom taught, and because the emphasis is now on ideas and not on execution, it is fashionable to take casts from live models.

I find this sad, as the rigorous demands of looking, understanding and interpreting are avoided and the figure produced is more bland and eerie than impressive.

Because it is normally clothed, the torso needs special study if we are to carve it.

There is a good chance, too, that if we look and discover things about its structure for ourselves, some of the excitement of discovery will transmit itself to the finished carving.

Life drawing is a quick way of looking and seeing. Modelling in clay is slower, and carving is the slowest way of learning how natural forms behave.

One short cut is to learn anatomy, as I demonstrated in my previous article (see page 6). This is no substitute for drawing and modelling, but makes it easier to see what is going on.

My account of carving the torso will be more intelligible if the anatomy article is read first.

CYLINDRICAL

At first glance the body appears cylindrical with cylindrical arms, legs and neck, but if you make a body like this, even if you notice grooves and bumps and put them on, it will look wrong.

The first will be a symbolic body,

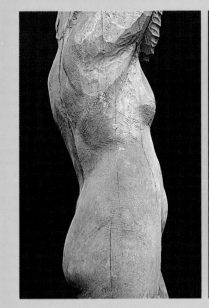

the second a symbolic body with surface decoration.

If after roughing out your carving you realise the underneath of the buttocks is lower than the crutch, or the armpit is well below the top of the shoulder, it may be too late.

If, however, you know the shapes of the pelvis, the spine and the hip joint, you will get the right relationship between the crutch and the buttocks.

If you remember the thorax is like a slightly flattened egg with the little end at the top, and how the clavicles (collar bones) and scapulae (shoulder blades) fit on it, the waist and shoulders will be recognisable.

If you know the scapula has a spine that runs across the back to the outside of the shoulder you will not, as some carvers do, make a groove that follows the inside of the arm right up to the top of the shoulder, effectively separating the arm from the body as on a doll.

Anatomy makes sense of the lumps, ridges, hollows and grooves of the body, but sometimes the combinations of muscles produce unexpected results.

Besides, variations in the positions of bones and muscles used differently cause changes in shape.

For this reason I have raised one arm. By cutting off the hanging arm at the armpit the shape of the relaxed ribcage is revealed.

FEMALE

The photographs of the carved female body show how putting the weight onto one leg makes the pelvis tilt and the buttocks change shape.

They also show how the different distribution of fat on the female body, the wider pelvis and less pronounced musculature, make the shape differ from a man's.

My purpose in carving this torso is to show how to carve down to the essential bones and muscles, and how to develop the forms to give the sculp-

Side view of a female figure left unfinished when I was a student. It has been out of doors for 29 years. The muscles of the hips are usually softened by fat on a woman. You can see the latissimus dorsi swinging up into the armpit and how the breast is flattened by the raising of the arm.

tural depth which an exact copy from life would lack.

One aspect that cannot be reproduced is life: the breath and the heartbeat. Nor can even the most cunning replica maker reproduce every pore, hair and variation of the surface.

You have to compensate for their absence by simplification and exaggeration, even when making a representational carving.

Having accepted you are using a different material from the original, and acknowledged you are incapable of copying it absolutely, you should resign yourself to being an artist and give the world something of your own unique understanding and vision.

Having said that you should also treat this as an exercise in getting to know the structures, so later you can take informed liberties with them.

It takes so long to carve a torso you cannot expect a model to pose for you while you do it. It is essential to attend a life class to learn the shapes of the body. Then quick reference to anatomy books while you work should fill any gaps.

If your own physique does not appeal to you, you could imitate the ancient Greeks and idealise the human

Front view of the female torso showing how the left side of the pelvis drops and the great trochanter on the right pushes out as the weight is taken on the right leg.

form, as I have done with this carving which is based on my own torso.

SYCAMORE

I used green sycamore (*Acer pseudoplatanus*). There was a slight spread at one end of the log which seemed suitable for the raised arm, so I could get a torso almost two thirds life size.

To make it as big as possible I left some bark on the outside of the hanging shoulder and lost a little width on the hips, particularly as some men are narrow there.

I used a simple way of scaling down to any proportion. For this method you need a pair of callipers that can measure the largest dimension on your body. They are fairly easy to make from plywood or sheet metal, or you can buy them from Alec Tiranti's.

You also need a board and large sheet of paper or a stretch of wall, and a long straight edge.

Draw a base line at least as long as the maximum dimension on your body and with one point of the callipers resting on one end describe an arc from the base line upwards.

From its intersection with the base line and with the callipers set at the maximum length obtainable from the wood (compatible with the other two dimensions), draw another arc to cross the first.

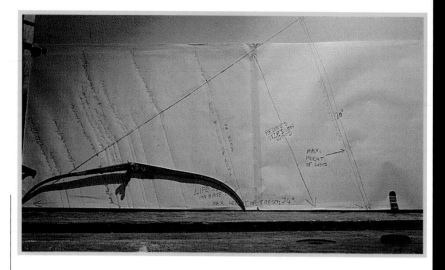

The method for scaling down showing the extended callipers resting against the base line. The base and long diagonal lines record the actual measurements. The short parallel diagonal lines give the scaled-down sizes.

With the straight edge you now join these intersections and the end of the line to create a triangle. It is easy thereafter to mark off on the base line and the diagonal the distances on your body.

MEASUREMENTS

If you then connect these points you will find you get a series of parallel lines. By noting what measurements they record you can quickly check your carving as you work in towards the finished form.

It is incredibly boring and will make for a lifeless carving if you take every measurement. Helpful distances to record are those between the anterior superior iliac spines, between them and the crutch, between crutch and navel, navel and bottom of sternum, and length of sternum.

Useful, too, are the width and depth of the thorax at particular points, the width outside the heads of the great trochanters, the interval between the dents where the posterior iliac spines meet the sacrum, and the width between the backbone and the outer ends of the scapulae.

All these points should be marked on the wood and redrawn as they are cut away.

You may not realise until you measure it how much the shape of the neck varies from the top of the sternum to underneath the chin.

You will probably have other surprises. In my case I was surprised to find the dimensions of the raised shoulder somewhat larger than my neck below the chin.

The positions of the nipples are also useful as are the lower edges of the pectoral muscles at the front, the latissimus dorsi and trapezius muscles on the back and the gluteus maximus and medius and the tensor fasciae latae on the buttocks and hips.

ROUGHING OUT

When roughing out the sculpture leave about 12mm, ½in, waste all around. In some places it will be more. If one arm is raised it is best at first to keep the interval between the neck and the body as small as possible to allow for changes of plan and accidents.

I used a chainsaw to quickly create profiles with the neck, the raised arm, the cut off hanging arm and the slopes of the spine forward to the neck and in to the small of the back. It also marked the hollow formed by muscles on each side of the spine.

I used an Arbortech Industrial to further shape the waist, hips and shoulders, but because the wood was green it was easy to carve by hand. Further roughing out was done with an 18mm, ¾in gouge.

Once the positions of major forms had been established I used a hand auger to drill holes as far up inside as I dared to allow the wood to dry from the inside and to reduce weight.

I bought a second-hand Hydraclamp universal vice, and although the carving was really too heavy for it, it did enable me to move the piece around more freely.

Without it I should have had to screw a block onto the base so I could hold it in a vice or with clamps.

I did most of the detailed carving with a 12mm, ½in No 11 gouge. This

● **Front of the sycamore block after chainsawing. The neck and raised arm are not yet separated. A block has been left for the genitals.**
● **Front view after further roughing out with the Arbortech and some carving with a large deep gouge. The auger used to drill up inside it is shown. Lines show the outline of the thorax, the right clavicle, the position of Poupart's ligament running down from the anterior superior iliac spines (heavily marked), the navel and a vertical line running down the sternum towards the crutch.**
● **The wood has changed colour after being left for several days. Detail is now carved in with a 12mm, ½in No 11 gouge.**

e chainsawn block from behind showing
oove for the spine, the hollow in the
of the back and the scapulae sloping
rd to the shoulders.

ck view at the same stage showing
 for the posterior iliac spines and the
ned by them and the sacrum. Spine
 right scapula is marked running onto
houlder.

e back at the same stage showing the
ated diamond formed by the
spinalis muscles from the cleft of the
cks to halfway up the back.

● **Right side of the chainsawn block
showing bark on the upper arm, the
pelvis marked, and the clay model
showing the muscles.**

● **Right side at the same stage showing
positions of iliac crest, great trochanter
and gluteus medius.**

● **Right side at the same stage. The
grooves around the gluteus medius are
visible on the hip and the bottom front
edge of the thorax is defined.**

Top Front showing further development of the external oblique and
pectoral muscles. Positions of the
nipples are marked and the left armpit
begins to appear. Only now is the neck
separated from the raised arm.

Above Lower parts finished with a bull-
nosed No 3 gouge, showing the dent of
the navel and the pubic region. Raised
arm is still waiting to be developed.

17

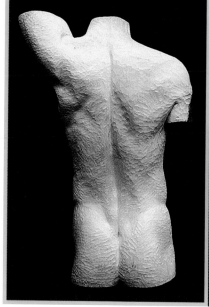

was used principally to carve across the grain working around the forms, but some forms were outlined with grooves first to fix where the lowest parts were.

Deep hollows demanded a No 8 or 9 spoon bit gouge of about the same width.

SURFACE

I refined the surface with a bull-nosed No 7 gouge and finally with a bull-nosed 12mm, ½in No 3. The rounded ends made it easier to use the gouges in hollows as the corners were less likely to catch in the wood.

Occasionally it was necessary to use a flatter spoonbit in deep hollows, and in one or two places I used a 30mm, 1¼in Swiss No 2 gouge flute-down to create a smoother effect.

On a piece of this size a very smooth finish is not needed. Indeed I found the worked surface more exciting.

Not only does it have a softer look, like skin, it also holds the light and shade and emphasises the modelling of the form rather than bouncing light off and drawing attention only to the surface.

Bull-nosed No 3 gouge being used to finish the front edge of the latissimus dorsi as it swings up from the lower back over the bottom of the scapula into the armpit.

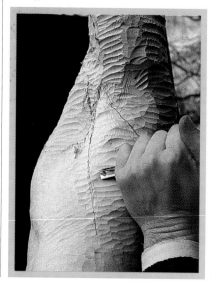

Above **Look for lines that echo or reflect others. The trapezius muscle is just discernible.**
Above right **The all important top view. It shows the curvature of the thorax, the angles between it and the shoulders. The left clavicle is in the front hollow on the shoulder. The hollow behind it is where the spine of the left scapula runs into the deltoid muscle. The slope of the spine of the right scapula to the shoulder is clear. Note cross section of the neck.**

Linseed oil would have made it too yellow, and wax would have been caught in any roughnesses, so I sealed this piece, inside and out, with one coat of Danish oil.

You will find consciously or, more likely, unconsciously, you are developing patterns out of the anatomy.

For instance, if you look at the photographs of the back of the finished torso you will see the diamond formed by the sacrospinalis muscles, that run under the aponeurosis of the latissimus dorsi muscle beside the backbone, from the sacrum to between the scapulae, and the way the inward slope of the buttocks is in line with the top sides of this diamond.

At the front there is a correspondence between the bottom of the relaxed pectoral muscle and the external oblique, and between the bottom edge of the thorax and the hollows of the groin. In later sculptures these patterns could be developed further.

If you do as I have done you should complete an attractive object and will certainly have great excitement making it and acquiring skill and knowledge which will prove useful even beyond carving clothed figures. ●

Alec Tiranti Ltd, 70 High Street, Theale, Reading RG7 5AR. Tel: 01189 302775.
Arbortech Industrial available in the UK from BriMarc Associates, 8 Ladbroke Park, Millers Road, Warwick, Warwickshire CV34 5AE. Tel: 01926 493389.
Hydraclamp available in two sizes from Tilgear, 69 Station Road, Cuffley, Hertfordshire EN6 4TG. Tel: 01707 873434
Or contact the manufacturers Spencer Franklin, part of Smiths Industries Hydraulics Co. Ltd., Windrush Industrial Park, Witney, Oxfordshire OX8 5EZ. Tel: 01993 776401.

Dick Onians is senior carving tutor at the City and Guilds of London Art School. Since 1968, as well as teaching, he has been working as a professional sculptor in wood and stone. He inaugurated the City and Guilds Institute Creative Studies course in woodcarving. He also teaches a part-time woodcarving course at Missenden Abbey Adult Residential College in Buckinghamshire. His book, *Essential Woodcarving Techniques*, is published by GMC Publications.

WORKING THE BLOCK

IN THE FIRST OF TWO ARTICLES, ROGER SCHROEDER FINDS OUT HOW FIGURE SCULPTOR ARMAND LaMONTAGNE ACHIEVES HIS STARTLING RESULTS

In May and June 1995, issues 16 and 17, I profiled Armand LaMontagne and featured his highly detailed and realistic portraits of famous American sportsmen including Babe Ruth, Ted Williams, Larry Bird and Bobby Orr.

He revealed some of his philosophy, how he goes about planning and preparing his figures, and spoke about some of his tools and techniques.

For these two articles I questioned LaMontagne about the details of wood preparation, making patterns, cutting techniques and tool selection.

I noted that LaMontagne, like many great wood sculptors before, preferred basswood (*Tilia americana*) for carving and wondered whether he had ever tried another wood.

He said he had used freshly cut white pine (*Pinus strobus*) which he dried himself. When it came to painting he stained the flesh areas to let the grain show through, but he had a problem with that.

"The grain took away from what I was trying to say. Basswood is the only wood I use now, and I don't stain it."

He obviously worked with some massive blocks of glued-up basswood for his life-size sculptures of athletes, and I asked where he obtained his blocks.

He does a major sculpture once or twice a year, so he does not need his own huge glue press. Instead he uses people who do it for a living.

"If I did this myself I would end up not having the right clamps and not enough hands. Until I find a tree that grows its own laminated, kiln-dried wood, I go to East Coast Lamination in

....

A glue press like this laminates the basswood blocks that LaMontagne turns into life-size sculptures. Photo by Ken Franckling.

Rhode Island where they have hydraulic presses. The cost is negligible when I know that I get the job done right."

The block has to be square. The company laminates a block with boards of the same thickness, usually 75mm, 3in basswood, so it comes out square.

SQUARED BLOCK

LaMontagne squares off one end with a chainsaw and hand plane so it rests evenly on the floor. It is nearly impossible for a shop to put a 2,000lb block on a table, saw and square the ends. There is no blade that big, and it is not easy to pick up a block that large.

The massive glued-up blocks are moved into his studio horizontally on rollers and then have to be set upright. This is done with a two-ton block and tackle that he attaches to a large iron hook sunk into a heavy oak beam that runs across the studio ceiling.

Even the largest glued-up block cranks up with a little effort. But he puts a steel noose on the top half of the block with a choke chain. The overhead beam does not budge.

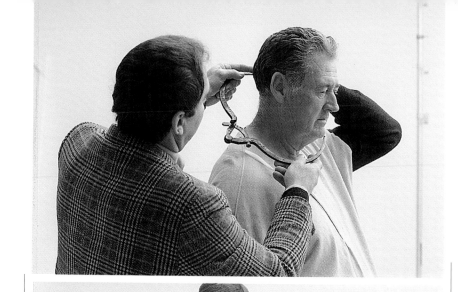

"I am only picking up part of the weight since the lower half is resting on the floor. The mechanics involved are not unlike what the Egyptians used. But I do move one of my work benches under the rising block so that even if it slips, the bench will stop it and it won't come through my floor."

PATTERN

I next asked about getting the pattern on the block. He usually works with a life-size portrait of his subject as a reference, and I asked if the pattern came from that.

He said, "When I can, I rely on photographs taken of my subject, usually from every angle. Getting a pattern from photographs is very tricky because photos lie.

"You cannot take a slide and blow it up to get your pattern. There is foreshortening. And therein is the lie. What helps eliminate that is to have the photo taken at belt level with a telephoto lens. This creates the fewest distortions.

"Even then the projected photo will be inaccurate. The camera does not compensate for depth of field, though the human eye does.

"Here's an example of the problems I have encountered. I take the measurement of a person's head, using callipers to get the outside distance between the ears. I then project the image of the body until the head fits within the measurement I have marked off on my pattern paper.

"The head is right, but the body comes out over 2m, 6ft 8in. The athlete is really 1.8m, 6ft 1in tall. If I projected the image so the body projected within the 6ft 1in limit, the head would

measure an inch too narrow.

"I have learned to compensate for these inaccuracies. This means I need dimensions of other aspects of the image.

"For example, I will have taken and recorded the size of the numbers on an athlete's jersey. I will use the size of the basketball or football my subject is holding.

"This is why it is so important to have as many references and measurements as I can when I create a pattern.

"So my pattern is really a rough sketch based on these various focal points. And when in doubt I go bigger. And I always go bigger. That is my insurance policy.

"To rely too much on a projector is a mistake. The projector is only a tool. So sometimes it helps, sometimes it does not help at all. There is no one perfect tool. It is a combination of tools."

The pattern is therefore not the most important factor in creating life-size sculpture, yet LaMontagne still uses one. So I asked how he transferred the pattern to the block.

This is elementary for him. He perforates the outline with a pounce

wheel, which is a perforating tool. He then takes the pattern to the block and uses chalk line powder which he pats onto the pattern.

The laminated basswood block for basketball star Larry Bird. A front and side profile have been established on the block that weighs nearly a ton. The cross-hatched lines in the upper part of the side profile indicate where the first chainsaw cuts will be made.

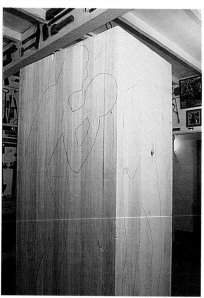

This makes its way through the paper and leaves an outline on the wood. Carbon paper is too cumbersome and too messy. This is a method artists have used for centuries.

FIRST CUTS

Next comes the question of where to start cutting away the wood.

Says LaMontagne, "Some carvers think that as long as you are cutting wood, wherever that is, you are doing okay.

"I think about cutting wood a long time before I actually cut it. I have to carve with my brain.

"Where to start has to do with how much wood I can remove in the shortest amount of time. It's being able to take a 200lb piece of the block off in five minutes with the chainsaw.

"It's not chipping wood away with the chainsaw. It's getting as much wood off as quickly and as accurately as possible. 100 years ago the poor sculptor had to take wood off with a hatchet and a roughing chisel and spend three days doing what I do in five minutes."

I took this to mean that if LaMontagne were slow he could be sloppy with his sculpting, and he agreed.

"Usually the slowest typist makes the most mistakes, and the fastest makes the least mistakes. The latter has an aptitude for typing.

"Perhaps this is why only a few people shine at what they do. It's having the aptitude.

"I often make these pronounce-

LaMontagne removes as much wood as possible in large blocks. Here he tackles the block for his Bobby Orr sculpture. (Protective gear should be worn when chainsawing). Photo by Ken Franckling.

ments about speed, but 100 years from now, the average person looking at my work is not going to ask how long it took to complete.

"The only important thing is whether the work is good or bad. Speed, then, only matters to me."

I asked LaMontagne to explain what he meant by the term panning to describe one way he uses the chainsaw.

He said panning was a method of roughing, of taking wood off a surface.

Below **The results from rough carving with the chainsaw. This is the sculpture of football player Harry Agannis in progress.**
Below right **Even after chainsawing and roughing with a large gouge, LaMontagne keeps the sculpture noticeably overweight. This allows him to make corrections in the position of the anatomy as he continues sculpting.**

He could do it with a roughing chisel, but preferred to use a chainsaw held perpendicular to the wood.

"There you have a thousand chisels at work. I slide a blade back and forth. When I get nervous that I might be taking too much wood off the block, I stop."

CHAINSAW

So when does the chainsawing end and the chisel work begin?

"It is when I go from rough-rough to finished-rough. Rough-rough describes the basic rounding and shaping. Finished-rough describes the wood after is has been carved to its final shape and sanded, though it still lacks the fine details.

"When the chainsaw is starting to bring me too close to the finished shape, meaning I won't be able to

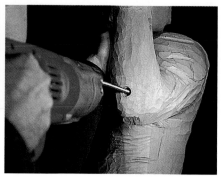

adjust the anatomy later on, that's when I quit with the saw.

"Remember, this is subtractive sculpture. If I were working with clay, I could make things bigger. With wood I have no options if I take off too much wood."

LaMontagne uses air-powered chisels only when it suits his purpose, when it helps him achieve a faster result. But this does not necessarily replace hand tools. It is just another available tool.

Asked if he had a favourite hand sculpting tool he said, "That's an easy question. The answer is a sharp tool. One of my favourite quotes is: 'A dull tool is the wrong tool'."

When it comes to keeping his tools sharp he does not go with the book-taught sharpening methods. No stone can maintain a flat surface, and oil makes a mess, he says.

He uses an aluminium oxide wheel and rocks his gouge back and forth on it to get a small burr on the concave side.

He then goes to 220 grit sandpaper, laid over a milled steel surface, and strokes the gouge across the paper until it is smooth.

The next step is the buffing wheel. He holds the tool vertically with the steel down and removes the burr on the concave side.

REINFORCING

I noticed with many of LaMontagne's sculptures that some of the anatomy looked fragile, especially extended arms. I asked if these areas were reinforced.

He said, "If my sculptures were like the real tree, there would be no problems. All extensions of the tree are reinforced with the grain and how it changes direction. The body does the same thing, with bones.

Left LaMontagne uses threaded steel rods to reinforce his sculptures. He first runs a heated rod through a bar of Teflon to make the rod screw more easily into the wood.
Above Driving a threaded rod into the bent arm of the Agannis sculpture using a powerful drill.

....

"But in a wood sculpture, the opposite is true. The grain does not change for an extended arm and there are no bones in the wood, until I put them there.

"I use threaded rods. A bonus with them is they compensate for the wood's expansion and contractions. The threaded rods actually stop that movement. So when the wood shrinks and swells, the rods make the anatomy even stiffer, much as reinforced rods in concrete do."

LaMontagne found he could not insert the rods with a traditional lubricant. Oil would come out through the grain and affect the paint applied later.

The solution was Teflon which creates very little friction. Teflon does not come in liquid form so he had to think of how to get it on the rod.

"I called engineers who recommended using solid bar Teflon. I could then run a heated rod through the Teflon.

"But I came across another problem. Even using a high-speed, powerful drill, I could only get the Teflon-coated rod in so far before the drill slowed to a halt.

"I realised that even with the Teflon, there was enough resistance to create a lot of heat. I was compressing air inside the wood and there was no way for the air to get out immediately.

"But after a while the heated air got out through the pores of the wood. Then I could advance the rod some more."

LaMontagne drove the rounded, threaded rod into wood against the resistance by putting two nuts on the

end of the rod and locking them.

He then tightened the drill chuck on the nuts. The only other way would have been to grind the rod square, but that would weaken the rod and probably round it over.

He also makes a larger hole where he inserts the rod so he can get the chuck below the surface of the wood and countersink the rod.

Once the rod is in he takes the nuts off and bungs the hole with a basswood plug.

SCRAPS

LaMontagne's sculptures produce quite a bit of scrap wood. He burns the small pieces and turns the larger pieces into mementoes with his lathe: basketballs, footballs, hockey pucks, baseball bats.

Scraps from the sculpture of hockey player Bobby Orr made 2,800 hockey pucks which he was able to sell.

"This is one of the reasons I take such sizeable chunks off the block. They maximise my spin-offs." ●

In the following article LaMontagne describes the tools and techniques he uses to get an accurate likeness of a face.

Roger Schroeder is a prolific writer and lecturer on woodworking, construction, sculpture and carving, as well as a cabinet-maker and amateur carver. He combines these activities with a full-time job as a high school English teacher, specialising in teaching creative writing and research.

PORTRAITS IN WOOD

IN THE SECOND OF TWO ARTICLES, ROGER SCHROEDER DISCOVERS HOW ARMAND LaMONTAGNE GETS SUCH ACCURATE FACIAL LIKENESSES

For my second article on American wood sculptor Armand LaMontagne I questioned him to discover how he achieved such realism in his portraits of famous sportsmen.

LaMontagne had often said in previous interviews that the faces of his sculptures were the most challenging aspects of his work, and I asked him why that was.

The real challenge of LaMontagne's sculpting is capturing the essence of a person in wood. This is Harry Agannis, an acclaimed US athlete of the 1950s.

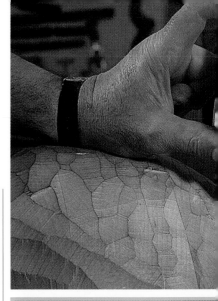

He said the most difficult thing for an artist to do was an individual human face. Not just any face, but a face that could be recognised at a particular age, in a particular frame of mind.

"Sometimes I see myself as a palaeontologist who has nothing but bones to work with, yet has to reconstruct the animal, including the surface details", he said.

For his latest sculpture of American athlete Harry Agannis he had to recreate his face with nothing more than black and white photographs that left much to be desired. From that he had to recreate the man, give him texture, colour, and put emotion into the face.

"The dinosaurs died 65 million years ago. Agannis died 40 years ago, but it may as well have been as long. It was not the ideal situation."

LaMontagne said the ideal situation was to have the real person sitting in front of you at the age you want to sculpt him. "That's the ideal, and for me the ideal is usually the exception."

He admired the work of Antoine Houdon, an 18th century French marble sculptor whose portraits were extremely accurate.

"But he worked from life masks. He did not have fuzzy photos to work from, nor did he have to put someone's face into a time machine and remove the years as I sometimes have to do.

"But despite the limitations placed on me as the sculptor, the head always remains the critical thing."

PHOTOGRAPHS

I asked LaMontagne how important photographs were in his work.

He said every sculpture was different and there were no set rules for what he did with the face.

With the Agannis face he had the black and white photos blown up life-size. There was one acceptable front view and one from the side, but he had

LaMontagne never met Agannis, who died in the 1950s at the age of 26. Though he was commissioned to do a sculpture of Agannis, LaMontagne had only a handful of photos to work from. But from them, as with this life-size side profile of the face, he was able to generate patterns and templates.

to alter the side view because it was not a perfect profile. It was turned 10–15° toward the camera.

From the altered photograph he made a template using an exterior outline of the profile.

"When I do a portrait in wood, I aim for a particular age, a particular attitude, a particular feeling that I want to capture in the face.

"There may be no photograph available that has all that. That is where the art comes in, but in the meantime there are an awful lot of engineering techniques involved."

I asked LaMontagne about those techniques. I had noted, for example, he left a block on top of the sculpture where the head would be, even when he shaped and detailed the rest of the body. Why not carve it to shape early on?

He said a block that had been squared off and given a smooth surface provided a canvas in wood.

The head was left until last, leaving atop the shoulders a squared-off block on which he drew accurate front and side profiles.

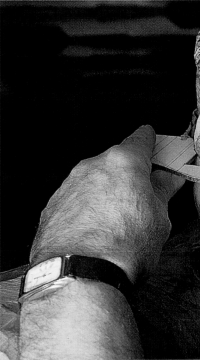

Top **This template, generated from the photograph, was used to check on the accuracy of the sculpted face.**
Above **LaMontagne devised this visor, held in place with a rubber band around the back of the head, to locate accurately the exact position of the eyes. LaMontagne's work calls for extreme accuracy.**

"This block is a precise thing on which I can draw my profiles later on. This allows me to separate the rest of the body, the easy part, from the difficult part of the anatomy.

"I cannot over-emphasise the degree of difficulty doing a portrait in subtractive sculpture. I have no room for error because I am locked in to

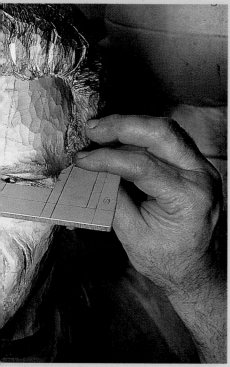

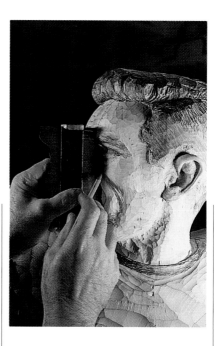

Centrelines are important, but difficult to create on a contoured surface. A profile gauge pushed against the wood provides a surface for the pencil to move against when he needs to make a centreline.

where the ears are going to be, where the nose, the eyes, the mouth will be located, where the back of the head will be situated. I am committed on all sides of the head.

"So to begin this task that requires such extreme accuracy, I need to start with a block that has 90° corners. If I know the corners are precisely square I will know where I am going as I remove wood because I know where I am coming from."

CENTRELINES

When I asked what were the key tools or techniques in doing a portrait in wood, LaMontagne said centrelines were the critical tools in doing the face.

"The vertical centreline in particular does what nature does, it divides the face from side to side.

"Nature separates the face into two slightly different halves. I do the same, and it is fundamental to my sculptures. Maintaining that centreline, not only vertically but also horizontally, is as critical as anything I do.

"In fact they are so important I refer to them as my genetic codes, my strands of DNA."

I asked what the horizontal centreline accomplished, and LaMontagne said the line went through the centre of both eyes. "The eyes are the centre of attention on any human face. They help provide that look that makes you different from Agannis or anyone else.

"I maintain the horizontal centreline as perfectly as I can. That is a very difficult thing to do since I am dealing with a rounded object."

As centrelines, horizontal or vertical, got carved away quickly, I asked how he replaced them on the wood, especially as the block lost its flatness.

He said there were two important tools for working on the face, a profile gauge and a visor.

The profile gauge had steel pins which, when pushed against a surface, conformed to the shape of that surface. When he pushed the gauge against the roughed-out face it provided an edge against which he could move his pencil and re-draw the centrelines.

The visor was a template which could be pushed up close and perpendicular to the face.

"I do it on something rigid like masonite (hardboard). The key lines I draw on that visor, which is really my gun sight, are those that locate the centres of the eyes.

"As I remove wood, leaving the nose out in front and setting the eyes back in the head, I want to know those eyes are going to retain the measured distance between them.

"Without a guide, if I am off ⅟₁₆in on the surface, I can be ¼in off as I set the eyes back into the head. If I am that far off, I have carved the wrong person.

"With the visor I can maintain that critical distance because I know I am going in dead centre.

"Before working on the Agannis sculpture, I took the eye measurements from the few photos I had available."

CALLIPERS

I asked LaMontagne why he did not use callipers to mark off the eye locations from the vertical centreline.

He said you could use callipers on a flat surface. That was how he got his distances from a photograph. But you could not use them on a contoured surface which was changing shape, as the distances would never be the same.

I commented that even in the rough stage of the face there was an identifiable person starting to emerge.

LaMontagne said he asked himself what characteristics made a person who they were. There were specifics you look for such as the shape of the nose, mouth and hairline.

"When I am roughing out, I try to emphasise some things in particular. The nose that helps make Agannis' face unique takes on some shape early on. Even if it is exaggerated or over-sized, the basic form is there.

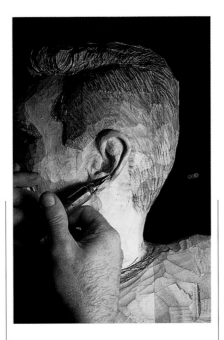

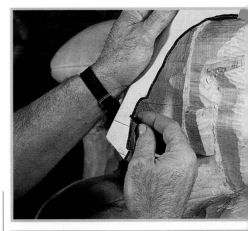

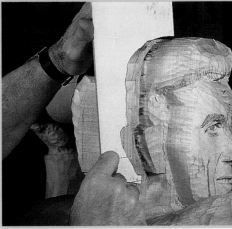

Ears are as unique as fingerprints. Here LaMontagne works on one of Agannis' ears using a custom-made V-tool.

"Ears are as unique and individual as fingerprints. And they are as different from one side to the other as they are from one individual to another, though at a quick glance they appear to be the same.

"I have yet to find two ears identical on the same person. Ears have a lot of character, so they are something I zero in on when sculpting the head. I even make templates of the side and front profiles of the ears."

TEMPLATE

I asked how he transferred the template profiles to the wood. He said he used a technique called chalking and rubbing.

"It's an old method, a meticulous and time consuming operation, but very important when you get close to where you are trying to finish up.

"I put pencil lead on the face of my rigid template which I then push against the wood.

"Here is another place where centrelines are so important because they give me the locations for my templates.

"I move the template ever so slightly to leave a black mark. I then proceed to trim the dark spots away. I will do this many times before I arrive at the right place.

"I do this only when I am close to the finished size. This keeps the measurements accurate in a mechanical way."

I asked why LaMontagne often

sanded the face smooth, even before it had reached its correct size and shape. I thought sanding would leave grit which would dull his tools.

"Rough chisel marks bother me. They are distracting and do not give me a feeling for how the face is emerging. They give a false look to the face.

"I break all the rules. I did not get into this business to save chisels. I sculpt wood to use my chisels and wear them out.

"Most amateurs are fascinated by having a large tool collection, but they do not know how to use them or they have to spare them.

"I am not fascinated by the tool. I am fascinated by what I can do with the tool. I realise I am going to have to re-sharpen my tools more often when re-carving sanded surfaces."

LaMontagne said when he was working on a face much of what he did was skimming the wood. A mallet was okay for the early roughing, but he had more control with his hands.

"I use a wide but shallow gouge for this and pare the wood down. Sand and pare, sand and pare, until I get to the finished surface.

"I am dealing with fractions of an inch. I have to remove the wood slowly and methodically while at the same time emphasising what makes that person's face I'm sculpting unique.

"Don't think I discount the body, because the body has to reinforce the face. There has to be an overall integrity, but the face is still the most difficult."

WRINKLES

I asked LaMontagne what tools he used to make pores and wrinkles. He said wrinkles were pressed in with a rounded tool such as an awl or even a nail, but it had to be very smooth to press into the wood.

"End grain takes details better than side grain. I try to make my creases with one stroke, but sometimes I have to re-do them, though I try to avoid

Top **LaMontagne applies pencil lead to the edge of this rigid template.**
Above **By pressing the template against the surface of the wood, he learns how much wood to take off and where to take it off because of the marks left.**

that. The variety gets lost and the creases look stale.

"The pores on a face are pushed in with a sharp object like an awl or a nail. This is tedious work, but it all contributes to the realism I have locked myself into.

"When it comes to tools for the head I use whatever works best. I found a piece of emery board cut to a point is the best sanding tool for the corners of the eyes.

"A long, narrow gouge does a good job removing wood from inside a nose. Or a thin file can work the areas between the teeth.

"It is not the tools but the sculptor using them and adapting them that makes for great art or mediocrity."

LaMontagne had a ping-pong ball on his workbench with an eye pencilled on it's surface. He used it when carving an eye as a reference as it was very close in size to the real human eyeball. It gave him a guide for the circumference.

Noting the sculpted look of the

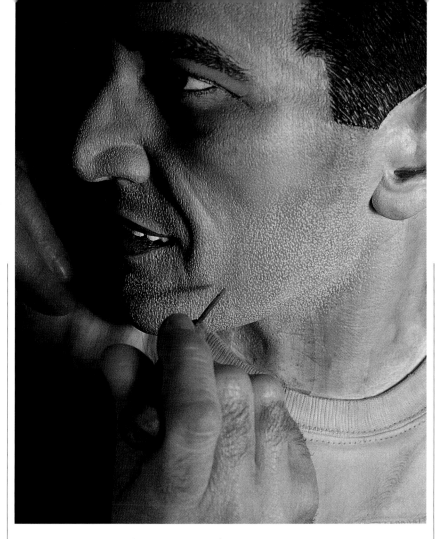

LaMontagne uses a variety of tools to create textures, including an awl to press in pores on the face.

....

hair on his figures I asked him if he had ever tried burning in the strands of hair as bird carvers burn in feathers.

HAIR

He said hair was important to a person's look, as Hollywood and politicians knew. More time was spent on hair styles than on anything else.

"It's one of those things that can change your appearance overnight.

"Hair is soft, variable, not an easy thing to duplicate in wood. But I still try to achieve a natural flow and you cannot really get that with burning.

"With certain feathers there is a stiffness that comes with lines that have to be parallel. But with hair there is an in and out flow. The only way you can get that is by carving it.

"That carved flow is more important than individual strands. It lends itself to a more vibrant look.

"Even though I do not like burning, I will do it for certain areas, say at the back of the head where the hair feathers into the neck. There you want some real fine lines.

....

Sculpting hair is done with the aid of a custom-made V-tool, which can literally split hairs. LaMontagne darkened the hair and eyebrows with pencil dust to highlight them, a visual aid which gave him a preview of how the finished head would look.

"Also for the eyebrows. When you try carving these fine hairs you are carving across the grain, and there is a tendency to rip or tear out the grain.

"A real problem with burning is that it produces dark lines. That does not help when you are doing a person with blonde hair. You end up using a lot of paint to cover the burns and you lose the fineness you were trying to achieve.

"Also, burning tends to make things look flat and shiny and too smooth, which hair is not."

To achieve the strands on his sculptures LaMontagne used a V-parting tool specially made for him by a machinist. It was shaped from high-speed steel on a diamond wheel.

This was one of his smallest tools and he pushed it by hand. It could literally split hairs.

"Making realistic wood sculptures is a process that requires a million adjustments to make a unique individual at a particular age.

"It is one adjustment at a time, and each chip I remove is an adjustment. Yet each is a final adjustment, because there is no bringing the wood back.

"You could say a wrong adjustment leads to disaster, but that never happens with me." ●

Roger Schroeder is a prolific writer and lecturer on woodworking, construction, sculpture and carving, as well as a cabinet-maker and amateur carver. He combines these activities with a full-time job as a high school English teacher, specialising in teaching creative writing and research.

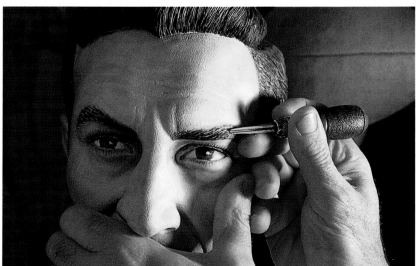

FANCY FOOTWORK

TED OXLEY SHOWS HOW TO MAKE BIRDS' FEET WITHOUT USING SOLDER

Carved song birds need good strong feet if they are to stand or perch properly and give a realistic pose. Here is my method of making feet from brass rod without having to use solder.

You will need some 5 x 2mm brass rod section. This can be bought from good model shops in metre lengths. You will also need some cutting off discs to cut the brass rod, a mandrel to mount the discs on in a power tool, plus some Milliput putty.

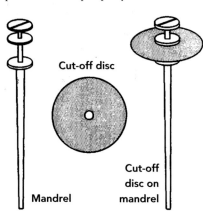

Cut-off disc

Mandrel

Cut-off disc on mandrel

Above left and above Finished feet fitted to a robin

The cut-off discs cost about £7 for 100 thin 22mm diameter discs, and a steel mandrel is about £1.80. Meisinger is a good make. Do not use a brass mandrel as these can bend. Milliput putty costs around £2.60 for a 4oz pack.

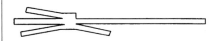

The marked up brass rod. Cut through the brass along the dotted lines, taking care not to cut into the area marked A

Mark out the brass rod as shown in the diagrams and cut through the rod along the dotted lines with a cut-off disc, taking care not to cut into the area marked A.

Cut-off discs are very thin and require careful use, but because they are so thin they make only a minimal cut between the toes.

A jeweller's piercing saw is the equivalent hand tool. Piercing saw blades can be used in some fretsaw frames with blade holding clamps.

Cut away the shaded areas as shown on the diagrams, leaving the toes the correct length. At this stage the patterns for both legs are identical and you need only turn one pattern over to make the opposite leg.

Cut away the shaded areas leaving the toes the appropriate length

Tarsus

The toes cut to length. Leave the tarsus extra long to enable fixing into the bird

HEATING

Soften the brass by annealing, or heating, until it is cherry red and leave it to cool slowly. This lessens the risk of the brass breaking. Then separate the toes by inserting a small screwdriver between them and prising them apart.

After heating and cooling, the toes can be prised apart. This shows the right leg

Carve the claws to shape with a small barrel-shaped steel or tungsten cutter with a cross-cut or hatched, diamond pattern. It is important to use a cross-cut pattern as a straight cut pattern can throw out sharp slivers of brass into your eyes or clothing.

Always wear a full face shield or protective goggles for all grinding stages as the discs are brittle and break easily.

Use pliers to continue the bending and shaping of the toes and tarsus, or ankle and heel bone.

Cover the leg and toes with a thin layer of Milliput putty. When this has set hard, carve it to shape.

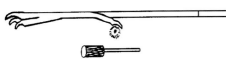

Carve and shape the claws with a cross-cut pattern cutter. The tarsus is long to allow for fixing into the bird

Finished brass foot before applying Milliput putty

Above **Larger feet fitted to a kestrel**
Below **Extra material can be added and textured for webbed feet**

If the feet are to be attached to a branch or other object you may need to put a small pin through the foot. If this is to be soldered on, this should be done before applying the Milliput.

Obviously, for larger birds you can use a larger brass rod section and cut it with a bandsaw or fretsaw rather than a cut-off disc.●

Cut-off discs and mandrels available from Bill Bragg, 9 Plowmans, Hambro Hill, Rayleigh, Essex SS6 8BT Tel: 01268 776409
Milliput putty available from Pintail Carving, 20 Sheppenhall Grove, Aston, Nantwich, Cheshire CW5 8DF Tel: 01270 780056

OWLING SUCCESS

TERRY MOSS TELLS HOW HE CARVED THE FIRST IN A SERIES OF BRITISH OWLS

When I was a child I lived with my family in a pub which overlooked the river at Ross-on-Wye, and I spent many happy hours doing what children do along river banks. One day I noticed some birds flying into little holes in the river bank opposite and I wondered what they were.

I went to ask my mother, but she was busy with a customer and somehow the question remained unanswered. A couple of days later when I returned from school I found a small book, the *Observer Book of Birds*, on the kitchen table. The customer who heard my question had bought the book for me. It cost 2s 6d, a fortune to me.

I owe a lot to that lady, whose name I do not know, and often wish I could thank her, for it was a parting gift and I never saw her again. It has resulted in a life-long interest in birds, a great love of wildlife and of books.

I have carved several birds at different times and am still fascinated with the range of shapes and forms that birds come in. I only wonder why God gave them such spindly legs, a real problem for woodcarvers.

Another problem when starting a new carving is reference. Relying on observation is fine if you are blessed with a photographic memory and good eyesight, but neither of these were given to me.

It is inevitable that observation has to be backed up with good photographs of the subject, so the collection of books containing photographs of birds and wildlife are among my many treasures on the bookshelf.

Some time ago I decided to do a series of carvings on a given subject, and I came up with the idea of carving the indigenous owls of Great Britain. The poor old owl has long been a favourite subject for the carver and has

Little owl with a squat shape and large head (*Athene noctua*)

The Little Owl in walnut with a yew base (560 x 190mm, 22 x 7½in)

suffered many interpretations through the years, so now it was my turn to pay my respects to these effective hunters.

The first problem was ascertaining the exact number of indigenous species, for the little owl was introduced in the 19th century and the snowy owl only occasionally nests in Shetland. So I decided the snowy was out, little owl in, with the tawny, long-eared, short-eared and barn.

LIVELY CUTS

My current thinking about finishing carvings is to keep the tool cuts. The idea behind this is generated from the energy that seems to emanate from the cutting tool. This seems to impart life into the subject and is the way I intend to produce all the carvings in the series.

There also seems to be a special quality in very old carvings where all the tool marks are showing. You feel the carvers have left something of themselves in the marks on the wood.

Much modern work is finished with careful sanding, wiping away all trace of the woodcarver's dexterity and personality, for we all cut differently with favoured tools.

I am not advocating that sanding should not be used, I've done enough of it in my time, but after many years behind the gouge I love that certain quality of finishing with tool cuts. Many old church carvings have a sense of life and movement, and I wanted to impart some of these feelings to all the carvings. The word used by bird watchers is the 'jizz' of the bird.

I decided to apply the cuts in a sort of sketchy way, much like drawing. Not carving every detail, but leaving areas unadorned to counter-play with places where detail was used. If the quality of the cuts was vigorous and it was not finished with great delicacy everywhere, I felt it would add to the sense of life.

PICTURE POWER

Normally I produce a working maquette, modelled in Plasticine, and because many of the subjects are difficult to see in real life, I rely on photographs, taken either by myself or other people.

I use them, as I suspect many carvers do, to provide me with access to subjects I probably would have little chance of seeing in their natural environment. Of course one photo is never enough, there is always the bit I can't find, and have to call upon my memory and imagination.

As well as making a maquette, I usually draw the subjects, either from life or using photos as a source to create the particular image I am trying to achieve.

This has two advantages. It helps to clarify the image I am after, but probably just as important, it makes me look at the subject. I find there is nothing quite like drawing to make the powers of observation work properly and get all the information possible.

It also helps to clarify the design and solve problems in the difficult areas of the piece. When the final carving is under way, it is reassuring if you feel those 'problem' areas have been thought through and worked out.

CARVING PROCESS

The first carving in the set was the little owl. It was carved in walnut (*Juglans regia*) with a beautiful colour and, being made from the intersection of a branch, had varying figure.

The fork caused a small problem towards the end with splitting, but not enough to detract from the carving. In fact the splits have become a feature of all the carvings, another natural event to add to the effect.

The base was in yew (*Taxus baccata*) with the ivy leaves carried down into the base to unify the design. I have employed this idea in the other two carvings. The surface was left with tool cuts, as I intended, and I applied several coats of an oil mixture which gave a dull gloss to the walnut and brought out the figure.

The second carving was the barn owl which was based on a photograph I particularly liked and developed in the maquette. This was then enlarged to give a side view of the bird and a front view, rather like an engineering drawing. This gave the essential areas of material, making sure it was in the right place to produce the carving.

It was carved in English oak (*Quercus robur*), a 300-year-old tree damaged in a storm and built up from

Right **Barn owl (*Tyto alba*)**
Below ***The Barn Owl*** **carved in oak and built up from three pieces (440 x 305mm, 17⅜ x 12in)**

three pieces glued together. The wood was still so wet I was unsure if the bond would hold.

To overcome this I glued it temporarily to enable me to carve it. When it had dried out I took it apart and glued it more permanently, and so far this has worked successfully.

The colour range of the wood was very good, from deep chocolate brown through to a golden straw colour. This colouring was the result of a fungus which produces the much coveted

Long eared owl (*Asio otus*)

brown oak. The drawback is the fungus can eventually rot the wood, and cause it to hold water. In fact it was so wet I found it impossible to stop cracks appearing when carving so I decided to use them as part of the design.

....

Sleeping Long-eared Owl in brown oak (560 x 190mm, 22 x 7½in)

I managed to get two pieces of brown oak from the tree. One was very good and I used part of it to carve the long-eared owl. The other piece was a little wetter, but had fine graduation from brown to straw. I decided to use it as the base.

The third owl completed in the series of five is the long-eared, inspired by yet another photograph of one sleeping in a tree. Of all the owls I have completed so far, I had the greatest trouble in finding good reference material for this one.

It took me some time to finish the first three, but now I'm over half way I hope they will soon be completed. So now it's out with the owl books and back to safaris in the deep dark places with sketchbook, drawing hand a-quiver, and the short-eared and tawny owls waiting. ●

After many years as a freelance illustrator Terry Moss now works as a lecturer in illustration, computer graphics and woodcarving at Brunel College of Arts and Technology in Bristol. He started carving in 1962 as a continuation of model making, drawing and painting. He also takes part in the annual Sculptree event, carving large trees which are auctioned for TreeAid. He is available for commissions at 10 Old Manor Close, Charfield, Wotton-Under-Edge, Glos GL12 8TS. Tel: 01454 260656

STONEWORK

DICK ONIANS COMPARES THE TOOLS AND TECHNIQUES FOR CARVING STONE AND WOOD

If you have carved only wood you will find carving stone changes your understanding of wood and your way of working, opening your eyes to new opportunities. It is also immensely rewarding in itself.

For the carver the main difference between wood and most carvable stones is stone has no noticeable grain. When you begin carving wood, grain is all important. You naturally carve along the grain, frequently changing direction.

But after only a few days of stone carving I found when I returned to wood I carved it as freely across as with the grain. I was working around forms and in better control of their shapes and was also getting faster results.

Many carvers in the past, including Veit Stoss and Tilman Riemenschneider, worked in both wood and stone. Grinling Gibbons, Henry Moore and Barbara Hepworth carved in both materials. It is a good tradition.

If you are trained as a stone carver it is frustrating to begin woodcarving because the grain slows you down, the chisels are more numerous and sophis-

Beakheads copied or derived from 12th century originals in various limestones by first year and part-time stone carving students at the City and Guilds Art School. The shape of each stone was carefully masoned to fit in the arch.

ticated and their sharpening so much more time-consuming and skilful.

Traditionally, people wishing to learn both skills have started with woodcarving.

Obviously carving stones vary in hardness but the commonest used in Britain are carved faster than wood.

Stone is removed in larger pieces, and because of the absence of grain and fewer tools, is shaped faster.

Nor do you need to be a giant. While it is traditional to use a heavier hammer or mallet, it is possible to produce results, albeit more slowly, using lighter ones.

Nowadays much professional stone carving is roughed out with an angle grinder and cut with a recipro-cating cutter on a flexible driveshaft or air line.

The pitcher is a thick chisel which has a flat end about 6mm, ¼in thick, slightly bevelled to present an angle of 75° at its tip. This is used for removing large lumps of stone.

The roughing out is done with a punch, although on soft stones this is not always needed.

The punch has a narrow chisel edge which has been rounded into a bull nose. Mine are mostly 230mm, 9in long but many are shorter.

The rough furrows left by the punch are ironed out with a claw, which may be a chisel which has had its end cut into teeth or it may consist of a replaceable bit held in a slot cut in the tapered end of a bar of steel, a claw holder.

Carvers usually at least have ones of 25mm, 1in and 12mm, ½in.

Finishing is done with a chisel. For general purposes 25mm, 20mm, 12mm, 6mm and 3mm, 1in, ¾in, ½in, ¼in and ⅛in chisels are used.

Carving into hollows is done with bullnosed chisels or with gouges, probably of similar widths.

The thickness and length of tool varies according to the hardness of the stone and the fineness of the detail required. Granite demands very stout tools but letter cutting and fine detail are carved with slender ones.

The tools are cheaper than woodcarving chisels although large tungsten-tipped ones are expensive. Tungsten tips keep their edges far longer than 'fire sharp' tools and will hold up well on granite, sandstone and marble.

Some tools have rounded, mushroom heads. These are for use with a mallet, nowadays often of nylon but also still of beech.

These mallets are used mostly for soft stones as they give a gentler shock. The mallets are round like woodcarvers' mallets only much wider.

Other cutting tools have heads which taper when new but are quickly bushed by the use of a steel lump hammer, usually weighing about 2lb.

Above Marcia Bennett chasing lettering with a fine tungsten-tipped chisel on a column which she has masoned.
Far left A good range of stone carving tools. Back row, left to right: pitcher for use with hammer, followed by mallet-headed tools, 2 chisels, 2 claw holders with bits and a bolster or broad chisel. Front row, left to right: 2 gouges, 2 fishtail claws, 2 bullnosed chisels, 2 straight chisels and 2 tungsten-tipped chisels. Note the tapered heads of the hammer-headed tools.
Above left Dummy mallet, small lump hammer and beech and nylon mallets.
Left The stoneyard at the City and Guilds Art School. Carvers work under cover with good light and air circulation. They sometimes use large blocks of stone as bankers (benches).

However, it must be said levelling the surface of a piece of stone by hand takes longer than on wood as only very soft stones may be hand sawn.

TOOLS

Another major difference between wood and stone carving is the shape and size of the tool are not so crucial to the shapes of finished details.

The stone carver can manage with few tools. The basic tools are pitcher, punch, claw and chisel.

Right **A block having one surface levelled by ledges drafted from corner to corner. Two boning blocks are visible on the banker. They were used in carving the corners into the same plane. The carpet under the blocks protects finished surfaces.**

Below **This piece of York stone was sold as Portland. It was a cruel trick to play on Gill Green, who has almost finished it. The iron stains show the bed of the stone. By making slots across the bed with a stone cutting disc large lumps could be split off along the bed but it blunted the tools very quickly.**

Light work is often executed with a dummy, rather like a small woodcarver's mallet made of soft steel.

Fire sharp tools are usually sharpened on a piece of sandstone (mostly York stone) with water. Oil could mark the carving badly.

The only way of sharpening tungsten is with a green grit stone or a diamond so these are increasingly used, particularly the diamond.

STONES

There are many stones suitable for carving. In England **limestone** is the

Above **This dragon, designed by Alan Llewellin, is having its side profile accurately masoned. He has plenty of experience so will avoid a square dragon. The stone is Maltese limestone which is soft and finely textured.**

....

commonest and most used.

Sandstone and **limestone** are sedimentary rocks, that is they were built up over the ages by particles settling in layers on prehistoric seabeds.

Some have marked layers which means they de-laminate easily and

Above **A life-sized head in alabaster, carved by Sylvia Worthington in a week. The red is shale and the white is bruised stone.**

....

therefore are not suited to carving, but others are virtually the same strength in all directions.

It is only when stone is used structurally or outdoors that the natural bed direction is important.

Some of these rocks enclose fossils such as hard pieces of shell and often have intrusive deposits of other hard materials such as calcite.

Above centre **Roughing out a piece of Portland stone with a punch.**
Above **Main forms being shaped with a claw.**

Above **A point being used on the marble carving of a shell by Lesley Powell. Note how it cuts vertically to the surface and bursts the stone off.**

These are stone's equivalent to knots and can be very annoying when carving detail. Sometimes there are voids or soft crumbly pockets in the stone.

Like wood, stone can have shakes, often caused during quarrying.

Marble is limestone that has metamorphosed under pressure and heat. It becomes crystalline often with coloured streaks. It is harder to cut and is usually carved with a different technique.

Slate is metamorphosed shale, some varieties being hard, some soft, but all easily break away in layers. It lends itself to lettering and shallow relief.

Granite, an igneous rock, is far harder but resists the weather longer than other stones.

Soapstone and **alabaster** are other stones used extensively. These are comparatively soft but present their own problems.

HOLDING

As with woodcarving it is essential to be able to hold the work firmly. A small irregular piece of stone will need to be cradled in a box of sand.

If one surface is flat it may be stuck to a larger block with plaster of Paris.

A wooden frame fixed to the work surface will steady larger pieces before final details are carved, but unless the finished sculpture is intended to have no flat surfaces it is best to start by masoning a flat surface for it to stand on.

For masonry all surfaces are usually cut flat at the correct angles and even rounded mouldings and columns are shaped by first squaring and then regularly facetting blocks.

If the stone is heavy enough it will stay steady while the first surface is cut. On softer stones a saw may be used. There are special ones, some with tungsten teeth. I use old cast off wood

saws, which can be bought cheaply in junk shops.

Other ways of taking off large lumps are to knock them off piecemeal with a pitcher or, more economically, to split the stone by drilling a series of holes and then driving in special wedges.

Another slow way is simply to draw a line around the stone and tap a chisel along it aiming it always towards the line on the opposite side of the block. Eventually the shock causes a fracture and a surprisingly clean break can result.

From this it is worth noting that frequent cuts directed into the stone in the same way can set up a line of weakness which may cause an important part of the carving to fall off.

To make a flat surface a line is drawn around the stone and little flat areas are made at four approximate corners.

Cubes of wood, boning blocks, are placed on each flattened area and with the guidance of straight-edged bars or rulers the platforms are cut into the same plane.

Lines are then scored between them and chisel cuts are made along the lines to create ledges linking the little platforms.

The rough area in the middle may then be reduced with a punch, making furrows at about 25mm, 1in intervals followed by a claw and then a broad chisel until the surface is even.

With practice the cuts become regular so the surface is gently textured. If it is necessary to make the surface absolutely smooth it may be scraped with a drag, a piece of metal like a large cabinet scraper, or rasped, then abraded with wet and dry paper of various grit sizes.

The carving then follows the same processes as in woodcarving.

RELIEF

In carving a relief the ground level is established. For work in the round

large pieces of waste stone are cut off using a pitcher or a punch.

Smaller pieces, depending on the hardness of the stone, are carved away with the claw or the chisel.

As with wood there is a danger, if profiles are cut at right angles to one another, that the sculpture ends up looking square.

Also as with woodcarving it is not sensible to carve the inside forms until the outside ones are made except in the case of a carefully planned relief when, as with wood, a drill may be used to set the depth of a ground and give a space for waste stone to move into.

Stone is a brittle material and has its limitations. Although large lumps may be carved off it in any direction, more may come away than you expect.

As with wood, if you carve up to an edge more stone may break out than you wish, so it is always sensible to work from an outside edge inwards.

A difficulty with stone, rather like that encountered around wood knots, is a tendency for some stones to pluck. As the chisel passes across it may drag up some of the stone below the cut.

This can happen if the chisel is blunt or if you attempt to cut off too large a lump.

Limestone and sandstone may be carved to a finish with the chisel and gouge or bullnose. As most stone carving is displayed out of doors and is probably seen at a distance it does not usually need a smoother surface.

Rasps, rifflers and abrasive papers are far more likely to be needed on stones that crumble or bruise too easily or where beautiful figure in the stone is revealed only by refining the surface.

Some people like to start with alabaster or soapstone because they are soft. Pure alabaster is hard to obtain in lumps in Britain as most is crushed and heated to turn it into plaster of Paris.

Some deposits have inclusions of shale which is very brittle and dark, quite out of keeping with the luminous almost waxy appearance of the polished stone.

The natural stone contains some chemically bound water which makes it feel resilient when carved with hammer and chisel.

It is less likely to be bruised if you remove large lumps with a saw and carve it with rasps, putting in details with cheap woodworking chisels. Alabaster also dissolves in water.

Soapstone can be worked in the same way but is crumbly.

Marble also bruises, particularly as one of the conventional ways of cutting it is to use a pointed punch which you hit vertically to the final surface.

This means a skin has to be left which is carved away with a sharply pointed claw followed by chisels and abrasives.

DUST

However it is worked, stone is dusty and it is easy to get particles in the eyes and lungs. Stones with silica or mica in them are particularly dangerous.

It is best always to work where a draught can carry the dust away and to wear eye protection, especially when striking the tools hard.

Always wear a mask to protect nose and mouth when creating much dust or using a poisonous stone.

For the beginner I recommend starting with a piece of limestone. Portland or Bath are readily available.

Portland is hard and may contain large shells but will take fairly fine detail, whereas Bath stone is softer, consists of large grains and crumbles on sharp edges.

If you can get one of the French limestones such as Caen you will find it a soft, finely-textured cream-coloured stone almost too good to be true. ●

Kara Belmont using a chisel to chase the surface of a copy of a piece of 18th century French acanthus leaf.

Stone carving tools available from:

Avery Knight & Bowlers Engineering Ltd, James Street West, Bath, Avon BA1 2BT
Tel: 01225 425894

Alec Tiranti, 70 High Street, Theale, Reading, Berkshire RG7 5AR.
Tel: 0118 930 2775
and 27 Warren Street, London W1P 5DG

B.I. Crawshaw, 3 Silverwing Industrial Park, Horatius Way, Croydon, Surrey CR0 4RU
Tel: 0181 686 7997

Dick Onians is senior carving tutor at the City and Guilds of London Art School. Since 1968, as well as teaching, he has been working as a professional sculptor in wood and stone. He inaugurated the City and Guilds Institute Creative Studies course in woodcarving. He also teaches a part-time woodcarving course at Missenden Abbey Adult Residential College in Buckinghamshire. His book, *Essential Woodcarving Techniques*, is published by GMC Publications.

PASSION FOR PANELS

IN THE FIRST OF TWO ARTICLES, SPECIALIST ROSS FULLER DESCRIBES THE DELICATE RESTORATION OF CARVED OAK PANELS AT ST MARY ABCHURCH IN THE CITY OF LONDON

I began restoring the pierced pew panels of St Mary Abchurch in 1992 and have been doing so on and off ever since.

First I photographed and catalogued all 98 of them, sketched freely to familiarise myself with their characteristic forms, and produced working drawings to scale from squared photocopies of my prints.

I had to confer with the architect, reassure the clergy, liaise with the police about parking, and move my workshop into the church at intervals to install the restored panels.

The process has been a protracted dance, waltz, jig, hip-hop and sometimes a limp.

Craft work at the bench is necessarily isolating, and contact with the world outside always vivid. Bringing the two worlds together is the greatest craft.

Mary Abchurch is a Wren church on a medieval site near the Bank of England. A dome on a cube with a spire, it is set in something like a Venetian piazza with an inlaid pavement.

The wooden-clad interior is extensively carved, and the reredos by Grinling Gibbons shows the pelican in her piety, piercing her breast to feed her young, a symbol of divine love and sacrifice.

Beneath the box pews the gentry kennelled their dogs while they said their prayers. The panels date from the 1680s and are by several distinct hands.

Authentic traces of the influences on native art, from Celtic interlace to Renaissance acanthus were carried in the subconsciousness of the English craftsman to be reproduced here. The church is indeed a treasury of 17th Century art.

OAK PANELS

The panels are let into the pews at the chest height of a man kneeling at prayer. They are formal symmetrical compositions of abstract foliage, stems, leaves and flowers, carved on both sides in 19mm, ¾in oak (*Quercus robur*) boards with the grain running horizontally.

The vertical uprising direction of the design is active and crisp, the lateral is passive.

Each side is achieved out of an effective depth of 8mm, ⁵⁄₁₆in, but through skilful foreshortening appears more fully three-dimensional. The average size is 510–535mm, 20–21in long by 180–200mm, 7–8in high.

After my euphoria at getting the commission faded, I had to look at each panel in detail, appraise the damage and face the particular difficulty. No two difficulties were the same.

Many of the panels were warped and twisted. In some the design was asymmetrical. I noted the tension of line and surface, moving everywhere in one of the six directions.

Copying from the masters was a traditional way to learn, but there is a great difference between dead copying, or reproduction, and emulation. You need to study as if you are immortal and work as if it is your last day on earth.

I laid each panel in a cradle cramped flat on the bench. This was a board with battens glued and screwed to frame a space slightly larger than the work so it could be held firmly with pairs of folding wedges. If the panel was warped I supported it underneath.

If work is not properly held you cannot apply the correct force to the tool.

For the repairs I used 18th–19th Century oak from pews which were being discarded from St Sepulchre-without-Newgate.

In the following account I will take a panel at a time, as I did at the bench, and give my notes on each, which should be read with the photographs in view.

PANEL 48

With panel 48 there were two missing stems. The replacements had to be finally attached to the original with slender glued surfaces, but carving them would involve some force, so the mother block had to be held strongly in

Panel 48 with the two missing stems.

Oak mother block grooved, glued and held in place with a wooden cramp.

place by increasing the gluing surface.

I reduced the irregular broken-edged gap to one with straight edges by paring them square with a No 1 chisel. I also grooved them.

Access to the inside edge for grooving while holding the fragile, slightly warped panel was awkward. I wrapped the panel in a cloth, put it in a wooden-jawed vice, and used a fine-toothed Japanese dovetail saw and

straight chisel to mark the sides, lifting out the waste with a small front-bent grounding tool.

I visualised the final result and squared and shaped the oak mother block, leaving enough spare wood, and grooved the edges.

I cut and inserted a false oak tenon and glued and cramped it using the gentle pressure of a Klemsia wooden cramp.

For this job I used white PVA glue because the surfaces mated well and it does not damage chisel blades. Cascamite resin type glues are gap filling but will damage a sharp tool.

After about four hours I began carving the stems, referring to the undamaged other side.

Whether simple or complex, good carving always depends on the clarity of visualisation in three dimensions, or four if you can manage it. Then, just when you are being carried away, there is the other side to carve.

....

Above left **The mother block fixed and ready for carving.**
Left **Carving progresses to match the original.**

PANEL 51

There was so much damage to panel 51 it was best to cut the panel in two and completely re-carve one half. As there was such a large gluing surface I did not need to groove the block edges.

My working drawing reproduced here shows the details of the design

Top **Panel 51 was so badly damaged it had to be cut in half.**
Above **A new block of oak glued into position on the remaining half of the original.**

7

6

5

4

3

2

1

10   11   12   13   14   15   16   17   18

Above **The working drawing for panel 51. The left half shows the profile to be carved.**

and the work involved. The drawing was done from a squared photocopy of my photograph of the original.

The photocopy and the paper were divided into a grid of the same number

Below **The finished panel.**

of squares, with those on the paper having longer sides. This enabled an accurate working drawing to be made from a small photograph.

PANEL 56

On panel 56 I made as small a window as possible to include the missing detail while maximising the gluing surfaces. I laid on straight edges and masked the window with tape.

I drew the design on paper with intersecting compass sweeps and transferred the cut-out, slightly oversize, to the new wood block.

Next I cut a window in the carved panel along the taped lines with a fine-toothed dovetail or Japanese saw and trimmed the edges square with a flat chisel.

I grooved the edges of the window, prepared and grooved the mother block and fitted a tenon as with block 48.

PANELS 91 AND 94

With panels 91 and 94 I began as before by reducing the gap of the missing parts to a regular shape. I measured the length of the edges, took diagonal measurements with dividers and transferred these to the new wood and cut a mother block.

On these panels there was enough gluing surface without the need for grooving the edges or inserting false tenons.

With the mother block glued and cramped up I painted it with white emulsion and drew on the design profile in pencil.

The central missing parts of these panels were reconstituted by studying the characteristic patterns of the surrounding panels. The drawn profile was lost as the third dimension was entered.

Carving is essentially vision, passion and force with tools. It is a process always teetering on the brink of implosion and dissipation.

It is vital to see the invisible, intermediate forms and to risk using the largest possible tools, which saves energy. A depth gauge can be used, but the understanding eye is more sensitive.

Chisels must be sharp as only

Below **Panel 91 with a mother block glued in place, painted white and with the design drawn on.**
Bottom **The finished restoration.**

The mother block was then inserted in the panel and the whole put in the cradle with wedges for gluing up. It had to be weighed down because of a warp in the panel. Then the carving could begin.

It would have been possible to carve the replacement part first, before fitting it to the panel, but I preferred my method of working in situ as I could refer to the adjacent profiles and forms.

From top to bottom
Panel 56 with the taped-off window round the damaged part.
The replacement block is in place, marked out and wedged in the cradle for gluing up.
The replacement block has been carved to match the original.
The finished panel.

sharp tools obey and free the force of hand and mind.

Your own discoveries are irreplaceable. The old carvers interpreted forms with freedom and panache. We see only outlines and shrink from spoiling them.

Outlines are important because they contain the movement between the planes which cannot ordinarily be seen, but can be felt and sensed.

There were traditional craft exercises for vision, such as closing the eyes and 'seeing' what the finger tips touched. Also for rhythm, by reducing a block in even-sized chips.

CARVING STAGES

There are established, common-sense stages to a carving. These are not my ideas, so they can be trusted.

Having transferred a design profile onto the wood you must begin either by stabbing down onto, or chasing around, a two-dimensional line. I prefer the dagger to the spoon.

Then follows grounding, setting-in, bosting or roughing-in, modelling and finally undercutting, refining vision and re-drawing the profile as you proceed.

I tend to see what is wrong with what I am doing continually and am driven by personal discomfort until the last stage when there is no more wood to remove and it is too late.

By that time the work has either become a whole, invisible to the restless eye, or not. At the end something is revealed, the inevitable result of thousands of small decisions.

Having been revealed it must be disguised. The restorer tries to discern the original forms and merge his work totally in them, but when this takes place he feels bereft if he has become fascinated by his own creation along the way.

His lot is to lose sight of his horse at the last fence. In finishing the wood to conform with the whole effect his effort is consigned to oblivion. Restoration work is successful if it is invisible.

The Mary Abchurch panels had been coated in Victorian toffee varnish. I made experiments with stains, aniline dyes and spirit varnishes but the colour did not prove light-fast.

Eventually I settled on a mix of black and red French polish over a dark oak stain, rubbed through and dressed with deep brown antique wax. It was acceptable.

INSTALLATION

The process was completed by installing the panels. With one I broke the pews open from the top, lifted out the top rail and dropped the panel in from above.

With another I knifed out the mouldings, which are integral with the rail, inserted the panel from the front and pinned the mouldings back in place around it.

Joinery in the 17th Century was by rule-of-thumb, not micrometer. The dimensions of either side of the pew frame window into which the carvings were fitted were never quite the same, so the panels had either to be trimmed on site, or the mouldings scribed to fit the carvings.

Each panel was a different problem to fit, as it was to restore. On site everything had to be done immediately,

Studio: 23 Rosecroft Avenue, Hampstead, London NW3 7QA. Tel: 0171 435 4562.

Klemsia cramps and Japanese saws available from John Boddy's Fine Wood and Tool Store, Riverside Sawmills, Boroughbridge, North Yorkshire YO5 9LJ. Tel: 01423 322370.

Helpful book: *Practical Woodcarving and Gilding* by W. Wheeler and C. Hayward, published 1973 by Evans, London. ISBN 0 237 44516 6.

whether I felt like it or not, with whatever tools I could lay my hands on.

Standing back and looking anxiously at the fitted panels the tension dissolved if the work blended into the venerable ensemble of the church. It did, finally.

Installation is not really the end of the process, nor even is the arrival of the cheque. The experience of one job may enter the next. Everything is in movement.

The Mary Abchurch carvings still dance. ●

In the following article I describe the carving of a complete replacement panel.

Ross Fuller was born in Farnham Royal, Buckinghamshire, in 1946, from a line of joiners and cabinetmakers. He attended Cardiff and London Universities and the Institute of Historical Research and gained a first class honours degree in History. In 1985 he gained his doctorate in medieval spirituality and religious thought.

He studied woodwork, antique restoration and gilding in private workshops before setting up as an artist-craftsman in 1975. He subsequently studied woodcarving and sculpture at the City and Guilds of London Art School at Kennington.

He has travelled extensively in Europe and the Middle East studying ancient sacred sites and the works of art associated with them.

He is registered with the Conservation Unit, The Council for the Care of Churches, and architects and diocesan advisory committees throughout the country. He specialises in restoration carving, design, sculpture and letter cutting.

PANEL PIECE

IN THE SECOND OF TWO ARTICLES ON RESTORATION CARVING AT ST MARY ABCHURCH IN THE CITY OF LONDON, ROSS FULLER DESCRIBES THE MAKING OF A COMPLETE NEW OAK PANEL

This article is a commentary on a complex series of actions and decisions which became, through experience, properly unconscious.

Carving, like driving a car, cannot safely be entrusted to the mind. Thought initiates the movement, which then passes into the body. If it does not pass, the mind will interfere and bring the action to nought, because thought is too slow.

This is difficult to describe, but every craftsman knows of its existence and explores it in their own way.

Panel 43 at Mary Abchurch was missing, so I had carte blanche. From the beginning my eye had been drawn by the panache of two panels on the north side, sinuous rolling acanthus forms in perpetual motion like waves breaking.

I chose the lesser of these two designs for the first complete replacement carving, which I installed in 1992.

I saved the greater for panel 43 which I intended to carve at the end of the job. But I made an almost finished

Below **The working drawing for panel 43 based on the design of an existing, original panel.**

drawing of it before attempting any of the restorations to familiarise myself thoroughly with their style.

I produced a full size working drawing from a squared photocopy of my photograph, changing the dimensions to fit those of panel 43.

The way you draw is a personal matter, but it is the conception of what follows. It is an investigation of what you see, not a description.

A pretty picture is beside the point. If you will not draw, you cannot see, and if you cannot see, what are you doing?

I am sure there are many ways to work, but this has been my experience.

At best, drawing is the contemplation of three-dimensional forms, four even. By representing them in two dimensions, we square the circle, which will be useful later.

Drawing is about bodily posture, relaxation and tension, a preparation for wielding the chisel. The cut edge must be as alive as the drawn line.

You must struggle with the drawing to taste the refusal of this live movement in your body. A great sensitivity can appear in this struggle. Something is distilled.

OUTLINE

Four years later I began to carve the panel. I transferred the outline of the drawing onto lay-out paper and then traced it over carbon paper onto an oak (*Quercus spp.*) board of the right thickness, which I had previously painted white.

After all that time I was impatient to start, but forced myself to stop. Before plunging in there was a chance to reappraise the design, to look at the heights, depths and intermediate forms, not just the two-dimensional profiles of the outline.

As soon as you set a chisel into the surface the outline disappears, so it is crucial to keep a vision of the whole for as long as possible so you can return to it.

With a clear head I tried to foresee what could only be done at that stage. I marked the centre line and final thickness of the edge of the tongue with a marking gauge while the surface of the board was still intact, thus establishing the vertical limits of the material within which the design would be accomplished.

The lateral limits were established by the tracing. The carving could then start in earnest.

Using mallet and chisels of a curvature appropriate to the profiles, I stabbed down close to the final depths, and in the case of the frets stabbed right through. I left 1.5mm, ¹⁄₁₆in or so around the profiles at this stage.

I used the mallet as long as possible, to forestall the descent into mindless dentistry.

SCALE

I moved over all the panel reducing the wood equally, doing the work of one scale before passing to another, not losing a sense of the whole.

The appearance of dentistry at this stage would show this sense was weak. I always used the largest tools possible, those which embraced the limits of the intended cut.

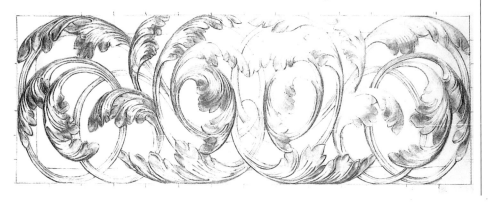

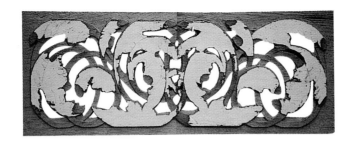

I cleared the margins (the tongue) by chasing along the edge, and by stabbing down around the forms and lifting out the waste with a front bent grounding tool.

It was important to keep seeing depths, not profiles. At a definite moment, I risked moving into the third dimension, losing the surface drawing and abandoning the safety to which the small mind clings.

I looked from an angle across the forms of the panel, not just straight down upon them as if they were two-dimensional.

I was emulating something beyond me. Appreciation of that fact came and went. When it was there I was learning.

A process of intuition began regarding the methods and approach of the old craftsmen which is difficult to put into words. With what flair and economy of effort they translated a linear design into three dimensions.

At first I approached Mary Abchurch carvings as art, which they of course were. I luxuriated in their subtleties, but as I proceeded my work became simpler, less emotional, more direct. I understood better how they were originally done.

I began to take down the stems, bearing in mind their overall linear movement, the unders and overs, the interweaving, whether it was rising or falling at any point.

Nothing is static in this kind of design, which is based on the observation of nature by generations of people who lived far closer to it than we do.

WHOLE

It was important not to forget the whole. I had to look at the whole sea and not just the froth on the waves. I looked, could not see, changed something and became able to see something else.

Thus I moved step by step,

Top **The carving at an early stage showing the drawing on the original white painted surface.**
Above **One side of the completed carved panel.**

....

inevitably towards a completion in which all the details blended in a unity.

Nothing was flat except the margins and they were tilted. There the carving ceased, or rather blended into cabinet-making.

The margins became tongues which fitted into the groove between the two sides of the moulding worked on the edges of the rails and stiles of the pew frame.

As the carving proceeded, I realised anew everything had to take place between the high and low points, that was within just 8mm, ⅜in.

I took down the tips of leaves which were obviously lower, measuring everything against the datum of the margin's ground scribed on the edge before carving began.

I noticed the angle of the leaves downwards tilt, breaking the forms down mentally and visualising the concave and convex.

I chose the largest gouges appropriate for the 'invisible' intermediate forms, Nos 3, 5 or 7, and worked overall, redrawing profiles where they were lost, and stabbed down.

These forms were invisible because they had recognisable profiles only in their unseen cross-section.

I had to avoid being drawn into premature detail. I referred to the working drawing for exterior dimensions, then separated the leaves from one another and pushed down the tips

and edges further towards zero.

I had to simplify and be free. I measured depths from the centre of the thickness, remembering what had to be done on the other side of the panel.

Observing, remembering and note-taking for this article altered the way I worked. Such sensitivity was bound up in the physical process of carving and everything tried to interfere with it.

INVISIBLE

Restoration must be invisible. It is said anonymous blending and intentional conformity is good for the soul, but if it were automatically so restorers would be the best of men.

I began to work more finely, restoring outlines of leaves that had been pushed down to their proper level, but had become distorted (fatter) in the process.

I measured from the working drawing to rectify profiles, and turned the chisel and freed my mind to find the flick and tension of growing leaves.

I had to visualise the relationship of profiles as they changed and avoid picking. The body repeats what it knows automatically as the mind goes to sleep. Then the body tires and the mind interferes, trying to do what does not belong to it.

Carving is labour-intensive, and as your energy runs out the work slows. When you lose what you are doing you must stop, rest and start again.

I worked systematically over the surface from left to right as a discipline when my mind flagged. I had to keep looking and see that everything was relationship.

The course of a carving is a sequence of seeing what is not there, and revealing it. The finished carving is actualised in the tension between the high points and the ground.

In the intervals of forgetting why

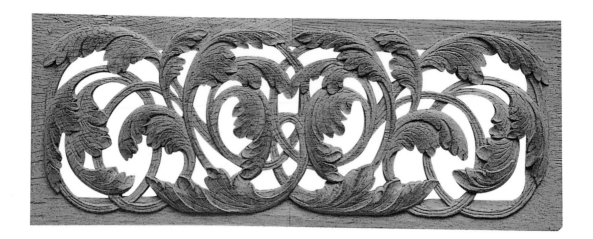

you are making the effort, rest on the fundamental techniques of stabbing down and lifting out the waste and of chasing the surface in broad sweeps to establish the intermediate forms. The meaning will reappear.

I used a few tools repeatedly, 2s, 3s, 4s, 5s 7s, 8s, fish-tails, veiners and back-bent gouges, to establish clarity and unity of form.

The confidence with which these were employed distinguished the old work from the contemporary. I could see the wonderful way convex forms passed into concave, which so puzzled me when I was trying to think it, before I found out how it was done.

HARMONY

I could see where the slow movement of the coiled stem sprang from and followed it round to the high point. Again and again I realised everything in these traditional designs was a matter of relationship and harmony.

In the wood it took place within 8mm, ⁵⁄₁₆in. Inwardly there was another scale. If the rest of me could not obey these quick perceptions, my work would be dead on its feet.

I began to work ever more finely, closer and closer to zero. Measuring from the centre-line of the edge, I feathered the panel's outer margin which had to slot into a narrow, sometimes collapsed, 17th century groove.

If one thing changed, everything changed. I had to adjust the heights of outer leaves to correspond to the new margins, and re-check the two-dimensional height and width of the carving from the drawing.

Carving on site was a problem, but I had to remember that either side of the window was not necessarily the

The other side, not a mirror image but a reversal of the design.

same dimension. I had to be prepared to scribe mouldings to fit the panel rather than the other way round.

I noted the way the outside ground dipped down around the tips and edges of the leaves and stems to give them extra height.

Redrawing as I went, I refined profiles and the rise and fall of the intermediate forms. I noticed the high point of the outer leaves was slightly lower than those adjoining so the design built to the centre.

This was subtle but made a big difference. I tested heights by placing a straight-edge across.

This lowering made carving the reverse side difficult as the panel tipped when downward pressure was applied, so I used wedges to support.

LAST STAGES

The last stages required an observation both intensely specific and global. I had to keep noting the sweep of the foliage and the force of its movement, deriving from the original carver's arm, mind and tool.

Bringing anything to a real conclusion is difficult. Usually you just flake out, but staying with it to the end, suddenly a unity looks back at you and you wonder how it came about.

Whether the result is good or bad, if the effort has been genuine you have participated in a mystery. Something is there which wasn't before.

But this was not the time for self-congratulation. I was only half-way through.

Next I had to turn the panel over and begin again on the other side. I traced the profile on the back of the

layout over carbon paper.

Of course it was not a mirror image because the design was reversed on the other side. Leaves that went under went over and so on, but it was a guide which I interpreted as I went.

In the case of this panel either side of the aperture was not the same, so I had to take exact measurements and trim edges, taking up any slack on site by trimming mouldings.

I could not do final modelling on the first side until the other side had been brought to the same stage, as depths could alter as I got closer to the final thicknesses.

Then I completed modelling the leaves on both sides (concavities and parallel channelling) and veined them and the stems.

Note the order of veining. On the fast side of a curve it was convex, using front-bent chisels. On the slow side it was concave, using small 3s.

The oak was brittle, but the effort was worthwhile. It imparted further life to the surfaces, unifying them, enabling them to be seen altogether.

If the edges broke I lubricated them with white spirit. I had the habit of doing this throughout the carving as it helped me to see the surfaces.

Lastly I undercut on both sides, throwing the forms forwards into visibility.

I am grateful to the architect Anthony New, the churchwardens Messrs Lowman and Henman, and the Rev Oswald Clarke for their support throughout this restoration. ●

Ross Fuller
Studio: 23 Rosecroft Avenue, Hampstead, London NW3 7QA.
Tel: 0171 435 4562.

WHICH WOOD?

GRAHAM BULL DISCUSSES THE MERITS OF VARIOUS TIMBERS FROM AUSTRALIA AND SOUTH EAST ASIA FOR CARVING

I am asked more questions about wood than anything else, what kind to use or how to get it to behave itself once the carving is started.

It is one of the most perplexing subjects but, like most things, it can be reduced to a set of basic guidelines which, once understood, can take care of most of the problems.

After all, any wood can be carved, but some are more difficult than others, and some are more appropriate than others for a given application. Knowing how to choose which wood for a project is the key to the problem.

The first thing to accept is there are no rules. It's a bit like the weather, every time the wind blows it's a bit different from last time. There are patterns and generalisations, but nothing hard and fast.

The same tree will yield wood with different behaviour patterns depending on where in the tree it came from. The shape of the bevel on your chisel will dictate the behaviour of the wood, as will the ambient humidity level. The variables are extensive, and so are the outcomes.

So, in an attempt to put it all into some kind of perspective, I will go through the most common wood characteristics you will need to take into consideration, and then carve a few samples from different countries.

APPLICATION

We first need to ask what the carving is for, as the end application will often be the deciding factor for choice of wood.

If it is for a decorative wall plaque you will not want a wood so heavy it will fall off the wall, whereas if it is for furniture it will need to be strong and durable and denser than the wall plaque. If it is for the exterior of a boat it will need to be weather resistant, and if it is to be highly polished it may need to be finer grained than otherwise.

Colour may be an important consideration, not only from the point of view of the surrounding decor, but also if the carving is a design with a lot of shadows, then a light coloured wood will show them off better than a dark colour.

From top to bottom
Jacaranda (*Bignoniaceae*).
Boree or true myall (*Acacia pendula*).
Malaleuca (*Myrtaceae*).

Make a list of the prerequisites for the finished piece, and this will go a long way towards the determination of the right wood to choose.

The next question is what kind of design is to be carved? If it is deep you should choose something not too brittle and prone to breaking off.

Does the pattern change direction a lot indicating you would best use a fine straight-grained wood that does not chip easily?

Does it have large areas without detailed patterns that need to be completely unblemished for best results, indicating a wood that scrapes or sands cleanly without any tear out?

DESIGN

Would the design be improved if the wood was wavy grained or striped in colour, or knotty or figured in some other way? If this is so, be careful the figure in the wood doesn't adversely affect the way it behaves.

Knots can be difficult to handle and may chip your chisels. Wavy grain can tend to make the wood brittle or prone to tearing, and heavily striped woods can have different density, hardness and grain strength in the different colours, making life difficult.

Is the colour of the wood important? Quite often it is, and unfortunately quite often the best carving woods for the design and the application are the wrong colour.

The best, usually meaning the easiest, woods for carving in Australia tend to be pretty boring as far as wood goes. They are figureless, straight grained and generally grey such as beech (Australian and Pacific Island varieties, *Gmelina* family), kauvula (*Endospermum medullosum*) from Fiji, or yellow such as cheesewood (*Alstonia scholaris*) and jelutong (*Dyera costulata*) from Papua New Guinea and Indonesia respectively, or light brown like bollywood (*Litsea reticulata*) from northern Australia.

In this region, woods with colour and figure that polish well and look great tend to be denser than is ideal for carving. Often the figure patterns we all like make the wood want to tear and break if we try to work them by hand to fine detail.

In some cases these challenges can be overcome by altering the design, or if we definitely want to use a difficult wood we may need to alter the way we shape the bevel on our chisel. This can have a major impact on the ease of working the wood.

It may also be necessary to carve the wood wet, before it is seasoned, as unseasoned wood is generally softer and more pliable than dry wood.

DENSE

This is particularly the case with very dense fine-grained woods like Gidgee (*Acacia cambagei*), an Australian inland desert wattle that weighs about 1330 kilos a cubic metre. It is basically impossible to do much with it when seasoned, but generally workable when wet and carved with a correctly bevelled chisel.

In the following examples I look at some of the species which can be carved from countries around South East Asia. They are not all ideal carving timbers, but they cover a range of associated challenges and each one has different characteristics.

For each timber I carved a simple eucalyptus leaf pattern, of the kind that sometimes decorates furniture in Australia. It is not of any actual species, but a generic gumleaf.

Each example has the same finish, two coats of clear artist's shellac, scraped with a knife, and one coat of unrefined beeswax dissolved in gum turpentine with resin.

AUSTRALIAN WOODS

I will start with woods from Australia. **Rose mahogany** (*Dysoxylum fraseranum*), is commonly known as **rosewood**, and the average dry density is about 720 kg/cm.

This is used for furniture and panelling and tends to be flaky and brittle where sharp rises occur, so the design needs to take this into consideration.

The grain is wavy, so to help stop it breaking you need to chisel it diagonally across the grain or along the waves, within reason, changing direction frequently.

A very sharp slim chisel such as a fishtail with a long bevel, giving a low approach to the wood, is best. Take fine shavings for best results.

When the wood has this wavy characteristic, the coarser the fibres the greater the likelihood of breakage. Rosewood tends to be comparatively finely grained, and this

reduces that problem.

It is a fairly gummy timber, and while this can make it even more brittle when it is dry, the natural resins enhance its ability to develop a beautiful polish.

Rose mahogany or rosewood grain, working and finish.

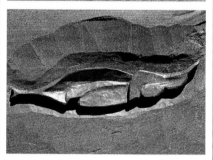

Silver Ash (*Flindersia bourjotiana*) has an average dry density of about 670 kg/cm and is commonly used for furniture and boat building.

It is not often carved, but it has characteristics that cover a large number of timbers, so it is worth including in this study.

Any timbers that are good for steam bending, like silver ash, generally have a long fibre which is conducive to bending. Short fibre timbers tend to fracture more easily. This characteristic can also make the carving process harder.

In the case of silver ash, it is a hard wood with long, wavy, sometimes interlocked fibres that tend to want to grab the chisel. There can be a lot of tear and it is easily splintered.

When carving, do not try to take out too much at once, either in width or depth. Try using smaller chisels than you would normally, and cut diagonally across the grain in the direction of the grain for best results.

Ensure the chisel is very sharp, and try a slightly more convex bevel than normal if tearing and breaking occurs.

Silver ash grain, working and finish.

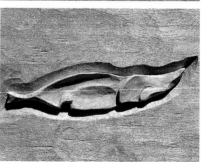

Jarrah grain, working and finish.

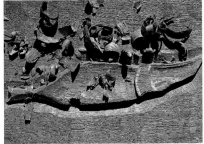

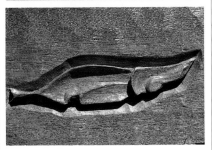

Jarrah (*Eucalyptus marginata*) has an average dry density of about 820 kg/cm and is a relatively coarsely-grained timber with slightly interlocked grain.

It is a general construction timber, and was commonly used for railway sleepers and fence posts and was exported to the UK for use as road pavers. It is now commonly used for furniture in Australia.

It is reasonably hard, splinters easily, but cuts cleanly with a sharp, well controlled chisel, cutting along the grain. It will tear out cutting across the grain, as will most Australian eucalypts.

If you are carving a large piece in most hard woods like jarrah, it will be necessary to alter the angle of the bevel on your chisel to reduce the likelihood of serrating or chipping its cutting edge.

Try increasing the angle anything up to 10° if chipping occurs. Re-grind progressively until you find the best angle that interferes the least with the cutting action of the tool.

An alternative is to put a secondary bevel on the inside of the tool, thereby increasing the strength of the cutting edge without altering the behaviour of the chisel.

PAPUA NEW GUINEA WOODS

Kwila (*Intsia bijuga*) is also known as **merbau** and has an average dry density of 850 kg/cm. This is a slightly interlocked grainy and greasy wood with a highly irritant sanding dust, and is used for furniture, panelling, boat building and carving.

The yellow substance visible in the photograph is capable of staining fabrics and concrete.

The grainy nature of the wood makes it unsuitable for detailed carvings, and as with most grainy woods it is best to test the design in the wood first before committing yourself to carving it.

One benefit of grainy woods is they often glue well, so if you do break part of the carving off it can generally be repaired easily.

Always ensure with grainy timbers like this that your design is not presenting a weakness along the grain, such as an animal's leg that might break off if any stress were placed across it.

Kwila is grainy enough to sometimes crumble to a coarse powder.

Kwila or merbau grain, working and finish.

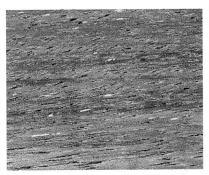

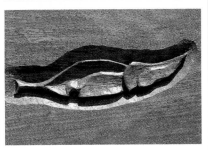

NEW ZEALAND WOODS

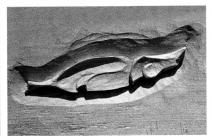

Rimu (*Dacrydium cupressinum*) has an average dry density of about 600 kg/cm and is a fine, even, straight-grained textured timber used for flooring, furniture, panelling and plywood, and is good for steam bending.

It has long, stringy fibres that tend to grab the chisel, like silver ash, and this can make it difficult to exit the wood easily.

It cuts fairly cleanly along the grain, but if you are not careful the long stringy fibres may splinter. Like many long fibred woods, Rimu is also prone to tearing across the grain, so avoid a design that requires a lot of cross grain cutting.

If this is not possible, once again try re-grinding the bevel on your chisel making it rounder or more convex than you would normally have it. This will help the chisel to move upwards out of the wood rather than digging into it.

Rimu grain, working and finish.

PHILIPPINE WOODS

Light Red Meranti (*Shorea spp*) is categorised as light by its density and is known in Australia generically as **Pacific maple**. The average dry density is between 400 and about 640 kg/cm.

Meranti machines well and is generally used for light construction purposes such as doors, windows, architraves and skirting boards. It has a coarse interlocked grain that tends to be stringy and spongy, and demands a sharp chisel to avoid its characteristic woolly tearing.

Because it is soft and coarse it has little substance and does not easily give a crisp finish. The ends of the fibres are easily raised when applying water or spirit-based finishes, and therefore need scraping or papering to clean them up.

Poplar (*Populus eramericana*) is a commonly carved timber which behaves in much the same way as meranti.

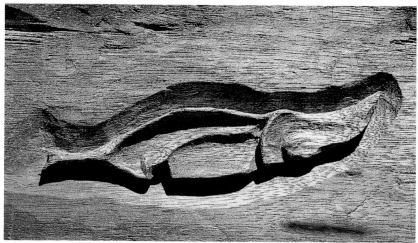

Light red meranti, or Pacific maple grain, working and finish.

MALAYSIAN AND INDONESIAN WOODS

Jelutong has an average dry density of about 400 kg/cm and was used commonly in the past for engineering pattern making. It is now also used for rocking horses, door cores, and drawing boards. The latex is used for chewing gum.

Jelutong is brittle if carved against the grain, and certainly is subject to significant breakage if used for finely detailed carvings, particularly with sharp or steep rises.

It has characteristic gum pockets that can be several inches deep and not always apparent on the surface.

With care, crisp and finely-edged carving can be achieved with Jelutong. While it's lack of strength makes it generally unsuitable for such carvings, its crispness and low density make it ideal for gesso or gilded finishes such as large picture frames. ●

Jelutong gum pocket in grain, working and finish.

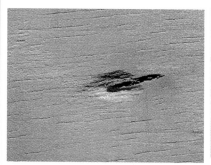

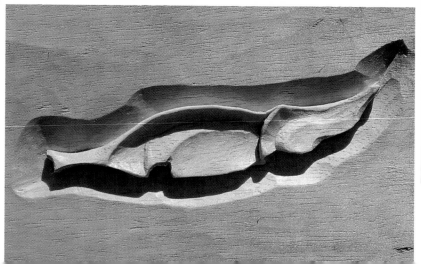

Graham Bull is proprietor of the Whistlewood Studio and Craft Barn in Sydney, Australia. Self-taught, he has been a woodcarver for some 34 years and teaches carving in all its forms to about 100 people each year, from schoolchildren and hobbyists to professional woodworkers.

GET A GRIP

DICK ONIANS' GUIDE TO THE BASICS OF WORKHOLDERS, CUTTING TOOLS AND SHARPENING STONES

In some cultures it is common to hold carving in the lap, with the feet or one hand. However, in the western tradition (when using chisels) the work is held on a work surface of some kind by a special device, leaving both hands free to control the tools.

Unless you are forced by some powerful circumstance to sit down to carve, you should always stand. This means you have mobility and can put your weight more fully behind the chisel. It follows that the bench should be of a height that allows you to stand without bending your back.

For relief carving a good rule is to have the top of the bench just below elbow level. For work in the round it is wise to choose a height appropriate for the majority of your work. The bench should be sturdy and not dance around the floor.

It is tempting to rush straight into carving without planning how the work is to be held. I have known students who have neglected this advice, and as the work has progressed the class has been disrupted by the sounds of carvings hitting the floor and cries of dismay, if not of pain. It is worth mentioning here that you should always wear stout shoes when carving. Sandals and thin shoes give no protection against falling objects, which may include chisels.

CLAMPS AND CHOPS

Countless means of securing work to the bench are now available. To allow for the use of a cramp (or clamp) there must be an overhang of at least 35mm, 1½ins, to allow a grip to be obtained. Room must also be left below for the tightening mechanism to be turned. At least one corner of the bench should be accessible so work can be clamped more firmly at opposite sides. Work may swing if anchored by only one clamp.

A clamp should be strong and have its heads in line. It should have adequate reach and ideally should be easily adjustable. If it has a fine thread it will take longer to adjust and is more suitable for metalwork. When buying second-hand clamps, make sure the buttons are not going to fall off.

The traditional woodcarver's vice or 'chops' is expensive unless you make it yourself, and kits are available for that purpose. The chops can be held with a

Student standing at a carving bench with the elbow level and body leaning to exert weight on the chisel. The carving is held on scrapwood by a paper join and the block is clamped to the bench.

bench screw which allows it to be swivelled. Naturally, this means you need a hole in the bench top. The jaws are lined with cork and felt to ensure a good grip.

A conventional bench vice can also be used, but this limits the angles at which the work can be held. It is always useful to have one if only for preparing wood. Vices with a quick release are more expensive but pay for themselves in convenience.

If there is provision for a dog to be fitted to the moving head, and if dogs can be fitted on the bench, then panels can be held without the need for clamps. This makes planing the carving easier as there are no obstructions above the work.

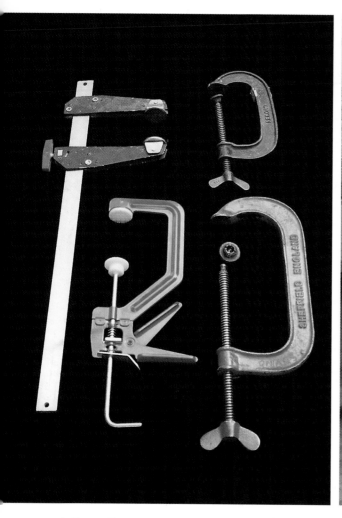

Above Clamps (reading clockwise from left): Long reach Jet clamp heads on a 670mm, 26in bar, G Clamp with loose button, single-handed clamp

Top Carver's chops with square block left under the carving to make it secure
Above Bench dog comprised of a thin metal bar holding a bench hook

Clamps and vices demand that the workpiece has at least two parallel sides. If the piece is irregular in shape at the bottom and can bear it, a rectangular or preferably square, block can be screwed onto the base, but the block and the workpiece must both be flat where they meet.

At least two thick screws are needed if the workpiece is to be carved with force. The lengths of the screws and their positions must be noted so they do not get in the way of the chisel or leave ugly holes on the finished article.

USEFUL DEVICES

Another traditional way of holding wood, which allows it to be easily worked from every angle, is the bench screw. The pointed tip is screwed into the underside of the piece, then the body of the screw is pushed through a hole in the bench and fastened by a wing nut underneath. The work may be raised by adding a block between it and the bench.

Large pieces of wood may be so heavy they need no restraint. They may be workable when lying on the bench or on the ground. A saw horse may form a solid cradle which allows the work to be seen all round and rotated easily. Webbing clamps are excellent for gripping awkwardly shaped pieces.

Increasingly popular today is the ball and socket type of clamp with the work screwed down to a faceplate which can be rotated through 360° horizontally and 180° in the vertical plane. The ball and socket joint is locked by mechanical or hydraulic pressure. A good one is expensive but very effective. It is possible to screw wooden bars onto the plate with sash cramp heads to hold panels or even to screw a carver's chops on.

An old device which is still available is the bench holdfast. This enables work to be clamped from the middle of the bench. It usually comes with two collars which are let into the bench in different positions. The largest readily available holdfast in Britain will clamp wood up to 250mm, 10in thick and has a reach of about 185mm, 7¼in.

RELIEF WORK

You can prevent a relief carving from sliding by using a frame which can be nailed or clamped to the bench. The panel can be wedged while carved, but moved around quickly. Alternatively a frame can be made on a board which is then clamped to the bench. In commercial workshops thin strips of mouldings are usually nailed to the bench. Another method is to glue a sheet of newspaper to a flat piece of scrap and then glue the work-piece to the paper. This is particularly good with delicate pieces of relief. When

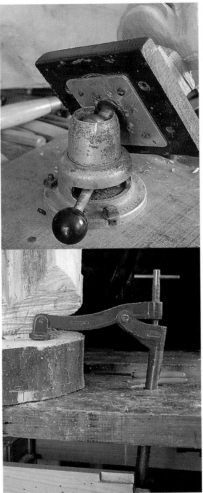

Top **A bench screw**
Above **Webbing clamp holding an awkward piece on a saw horse**

Top **Ball and socket clamp with home-made faceplate. Work is screwed on from underneath**
Above **Holdfast in use**

Above **Tirolean carving horse from the carving school at St Jakob**

finished, the carving is gently prised off with a broad straight-edged chisel. You can also use double-sided tape.

Many carvers have their own solutions to the problem of holding. I once saw a good example at a carving school in the South Tirol. It was a simple horse with a carving table held against a post by a threaded bar with a handle. This passed through a slot in the post and allowed the table to be raised or lowered and tilted. The work was fastened to the table by a bench screw so it could be rotated.

ANCHORING FOR ADHESION

Holding is important whenever you need to glue wood, whether building up a block before carving or repairing a break. In the latter case, the surface is often irregular or in danger of being bruised by the head of a clamp.

An old furniture restorer's trick is to cut sections out of an old bed spring and straighten them out to form rings. The cutting usually leaves the end of the metal sharp and when the ring is opened out it will grip on an uneven surface. But beware, this will leave a mark unless the wood is protected.

The Jet Clamp is another useful device which will grip on an uneven surface, and because the heads can be loosened, the surfaces do not need to be parallel. In addition, the heads have rubber pads which reduce the risk of bruising and slipping.

The cam clamp has wooden jaws with cork padding. This is quickly adjusted and has a soft grip, useful on delicate objects. The single-handed clamp derived from the mastic gun is cheap and effective too. It does not exert as much pressure as a G clamp

but is it good for light work or in conjunction with another clamp.

TOOLS AND ACCESSORIES

Once the work-piece is firmly anchored, you need chisels and a mallet. Carvers' mallets are round. The best are made of *lignum vitae* as even a 50mm, 2in diameter model will be quite weighty and last well. They are also made of beech (*Fagus spp*), apple (*Malus sylvestris*) or other tough woods. A soft steel dummy used for delicate stone carving may also be used.

Rasps and rifflers are useful accessories. Handcut ones last longer and cut well. Surforms and dreadnoughts also help in shaping regular curves especially on end grain. But they are all best followed with a chisel finish as they can scratch the work deeply. The alternative is the lengthy, boring and

Above **Bed spring clamp holding part of a badly damaged outdoor sculpture**

Top right **Jet clamp showing the head fitting well on an angled surface**
Above right **JA cam clamp**

detail-blurring process of sandpapering down through several grades of paper.

There are now many machines available to speed up the work: chainsaws, bandsaws and rotary discs, burrs and sanders attached directly to drills or on flexible drive shafts which can rough out and finish carvings particularly in difficult corners. The effects they produce are different from those left by chisels, often less attractive. They are also expensive, noisy, dusty and less safe.

SHARPENING STONES

It is impossible to carve well without sharp tools. Equipment for sharpening should be bought with the first chisel. When starting out, unless you have access to a grinder and a buffing machine, sharpening has to be done the hard way by hand. You will need a coarse stone, a medium stone and a finishing stone to hand.

Oil stones are most commonly used. The usual size of a bench stone is 8in, 200mm long by 2in, 50mm wide. The synthetic and slate stones are 1in, 25mm thick but hard Arkansas, which is the best finishing stone, is very expensive and is now usually ½in, 13mm thick. The coarse and medium stones may be bought as a combination stone, coarse on one side and medium on the other. The orange, India stone is an excellent medium stone. The cheaper oil stones are too soft to last.

Twenty years ago there were clearly differentiated Washita and Arkansas stones. Although of the same mineral from the same source in the Washita mountains in Arkansas, the Washita stone looks porous and is much softer.

Now, perhaps because Arkansas is a well known name, the cheaper stone is also labelled Arkansas and the unwary purchaser may buy the poorer kind by mistake. Genuine hard Arkansas is difficult to find. It is translucent, particularly when wetted. Washita stone is not. The black stone seems slightly faster cutting, producing a better edge, than the hard white Arkansas. It is not translucent. Hard Arkansas stones last more than a lifetime unless dropped.

In addition to the bench stones, you need at least one fine (preferably Arkansas) slip stone. Slips come in various shapes and sizes. The rule is to make sure you have one which will fit inside your smallest gouge. It will do for your big ones too, although you may prefer to have different thicknesses for wider tools.

I like to grind an inside bevel on most of my straight gouges, but even if you do not want this bevel you may at some time be forced to grind inside. Therefore, keeping a carborundum or India slip as well will save time.

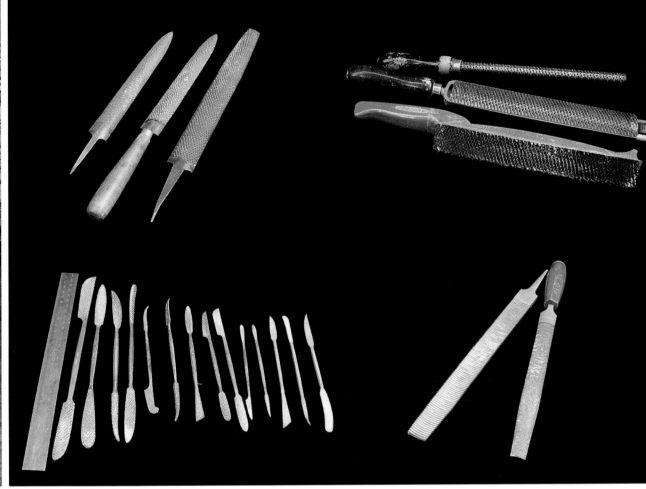

Top right **Rasps: the two on the left are hand cut and typically pointed. The other is a standard half round bastard rasp**

Above **Assorted handmade rifflers shown against a 305mm, 12in ruler**

Top **Three surform rasps: standard flat, half round and the very useful Roundfile**
Above **A dreadnought and a half round Aven Trimmerfile**

SAVING ON STONES

There are various ways of saving money. A biggish Arkansas slip stone can be made to double as a bench stone if it is set into a block of wood. Slate bench and slip stones are adequate for finishing. They are cheap but cut the metal very slowly. Also particles of grit or bits of discarded burr can get caught in the surface and scratch the chisel's edge.

Japanese water stones are excellent at removing the metal, indeed the finishing stones quickly produce as good an edge as an Arkansas. They are comparatively cheap. They work on the principle that the surface is constantly worn away to expose fresh sharp grit.

Another disadvantage is that you need to dry the tools thoroughly, and any oil that finds its way onto the stone spoils it. For finishing carving chisels a 6, 000 grit stone is quite sufficient and

is far cheaper than the 8, 000 grit stone. The slip stones tend to wear into bumps and constantly need reshaping.

Removing the burr after sharpening and keeping the edge keen are best done on a leather strop. A piece of hide will burnish the metal eventually but a dressing of chrome polish such as Solvol Autosol or Autoglym which can be bought from car or motorcycle accessory shops quickly removes the burr and polishes the metal to a mirror finish and the keenest edge.

When the paste dries out it falls off the leather so it is best to rub some tallow or vaseline into the flesh side of the leather and then smear the abrasive paste in afterwards. A little will then last a long time.

In acquiring equipment it is a false economy and can be very frustrating to buy second rate stuff. It is better to start with a small selection of good tools. ●

Dick Onians is head of the carving department of the City and Guilds of London Art School. Since 1968, as well as teaching, he has been working as a professional sculptor in wood and stone. He inaugurated the City and Guilds Institute Creative Studies course in Woodcarving.

THE GREAT AUSTRALIAN BIGHT

PETER FLETCHER SHOWS HOW TO GET YOUR TEETH INTO CARVING TAGUA NUTS

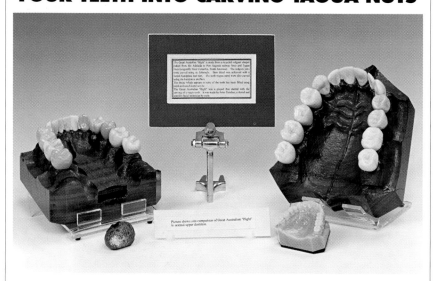

The idea for this project, *The Great Australian Bight*, came to me after I had carved a single tooth in olivewood (*Notelaea lingustrian*). To make a complete set of teeth I set about trying to find the whitest wood available locally.

From previous woodturning projects I knew red river gum (*Eucalyptus camaldulensis*) would be suitable for the jaws, and this had a variety of colour variations.

I experimented with many light-coloured woods, including olivewood, Huon pine (*Dacrydium franklinii*), acacia (*Acacia cambagei*) and bottle brush, or tea tree (*Melaleuca leucadendron*).

The completed Great Australian Bight, tagua nut and normal false teeth for size comparison.

I eventually came across some tagua nuts(*Phytelephas macrocarpa*) which had a design carved on them. This carving revealed what I was looking for.

Tagua nuts are native to Columbia, Ecuador and Peru in South America.

The size of these teeth is approximately seven times normal dentition. Therefore, allowance had to be made for selection of the tagua nuts suitable for the teeth to be carved.

A single upper central is about the same size as your thumb to the first joint.

When selecting the nuts I had to first grind part of the protective shell away to reveal the colour underneath. I bought twice as many nuts as I needed so I could find the whitest, creamiest to closely

Great Australian Bight, articulated.

resemble a normal tooth.

I bought the tagua nuts by mail order from Supreme Wood at St Albans in Victoria, Australia.

GRINDING

Once I decided which tooth was to be carved and the nut which would suit, I began to reduce the size by grinding a rough shape using a belt sander. I find this is the fastest method and gives me more control as I visualise the tooth taking shape.

One problem I encountered while grinding tagua nuts was the very fine dust created. It is essential to wear a mask and visor if an extraction system is not installed.

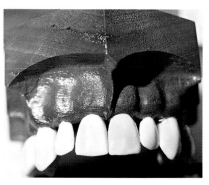

Close up of upper teeth and gums.

Once the roughing was completed I began shaping in more detail, using a suspension motor, handpiece and tungsten carbide dental burrs.

A lot of the anatomy of the tooth was from memory but I occasionally referred to a dental workshop manual for particular landmarks.

The tagua nut is ideal for carving using burrs because it is very hard and dense with no grain as such to worry about. On close examination there are growth rings but these are close together so it makes carving easy.

I now appreciate why the native South Americans used tagua nuts in the past for carving buttons, chessmen and dice as a substitute for ivory.

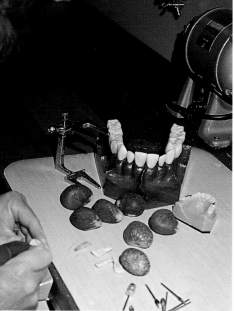

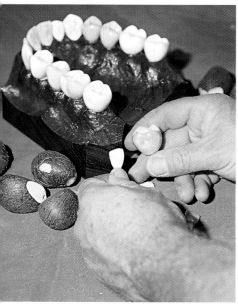

From top to bottom
Preparation of the jaws using the belt sander.
Carving a tooth with the burrs and handpiece.
Comparison of normal and tagua nut teeth.

CAVITY

The nut itself is not completely solid but has a cavity in the centre which can pose a problem. Depending on which tooth is to be carved, I overcame this by making a feature of the cavity and filling it with tooth coloured dental acrylic which was cured in a dental hydroflask (small pressure cooker).

Once the acrylic had cured I was able to continue carving the detail, and when complete the tooth appeared to have had a filling.

At this stage I prepared the upper and lower jaws. These were made from an old redgum railway sleeper salvaged from the Adelaide to Port Augusta railway line in South Australia.

I was able to purchase this sleeper from the Railway Sleeper Company at Reynella in Adelaide, South Australia.

To construct the jaws I first used an Arbortech rotary cutter fitted to my angle grinder. This was ideal for removing the initial waste and shaping some of the detail.

The more intricate carving was achieved using the handpiece and burrs once again. Extra care was needed when setting the teeth in the arches so the mesial (middle) and distal (outer) surfaces would contact each other.

On this project I completed all the upper teeth and jaws before attempting the lower. When I was satisfied with each tooth's detail I polished the nut with dental pumice and tripoli.

Because of the hardness of the nut, the burr marks were removed by the pumice and the surface remained smooth.

ARTICULATED

I then began the lower arch and tagua teeth and completed them to suit the opposing upper dentition. Some allowances had to made when articulating the jaws together by grinding the occlusal surfaces, that js the surfaces of the teeth when closed together.

The plain line articulator was modified to suit the oversize jaws, then

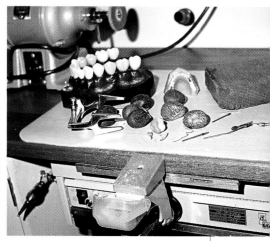

The tools and materials used for the project. There is a dust extraction vacuum unit below the bench.

sandblasted and polished. I also sandblasted the tissue areas of the redgum jaws to achieve a dull and more natural looking effect. The top, bottom and sides were fine sanded and finished smooth.

I then gave the tagua teeth a coat of clear gloss enamel to protect them from discolouring. I gave the jaws coats of satin for the tissue areas and full gloss for the top, bottom and sides.

The final stage was drilling, positioning and cementing the teeth in situ.

I added a plaque and furniture tacks to protect the base and top, and The Great Australian Bight was complete. ●

Peter Fletcher is a dental and maxillo-facial technician by trade. He enjoys woodturning and woodcarving and makes a feature of his work with the addition of coloured acrylic which adds character to projects.

Arbortech supplied in the UK by BriMarc Associates, 8 Ladbroke Park, Millers Road, Warwick CV34 5AE.
Tel: 01926 493389.

CHAIN REACTIONS

JOHN BEASLEY SAYS A CHAINSAW CAN BE USED SAFELY AND EFFECTIVELY FOR WOODCARVING, BUT HE STRESSES THAT VIGILANCE IS ALWAYS ESSENTIAL

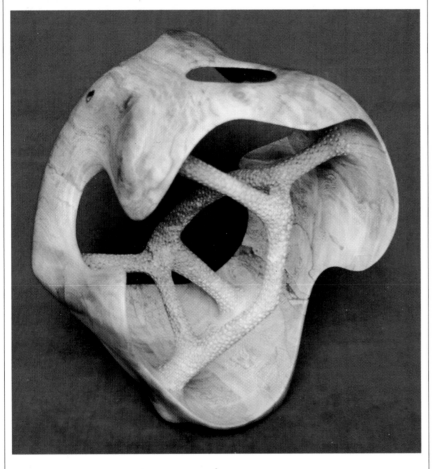

Before I start, I must emphasise that the benefits of using the chainsaw come at a cost – constant vigilance. Although it is a wonderful tool, it can also inflict severe injuries. Most chainsaws on sale today come with detailed instruction manuals, and these should be read and understood if you are new to the tool. Take time to develop confidence and a feel for your saw before attempting more difficult techniques.

The techniques I describe here have been developed over time, and with experience I have become confident in using them. However, someone new to the chainsaw may encounter difficulties I do not mention. So although I have tried to describe as clearly as I can what I do and the likely safety implications, it remains your responsibility to use the chainsaw with caution at all times. In particular, remember that if the upper part of the nose comes in contact with an object, it will cause kickback.

STRAIGHT CUTS

Chainsaws are designed to make straight cuts through timber; the flat bar more or less dictates this. (Sometimes a badly sharpened saw, or one with damage to one side of the teeth, will cut in a curve, often jamming in the cut as the curve tightens.) Straight line cutting is useful for removing large blocks, squaring the base of the sculpture, and so on, but it takes one only so far.

As a sculptor, I remove the bumper spike from my chainsaw, partly because of the damage it can do to an almost completed piece, but also because I can produce a more accurate straight cut without it. This is because

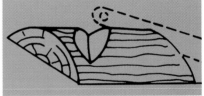

Two straight cuts can meet to remove a wedge of timber

levering the saw through the wood using the spike also causes some sideways twisting movement which is inclined to skew the cut.

Two intersecting straight cuts can be used to remove a wedge of timber, though it takes practice to get the cuts to meet accurately. This is a good time to develop the skill of watching both ends of the bar as the cut proceeds. If you focus on one end only, the other end is likely to cut too deep, perhaps ruining the whole project.

Keep a mental 'no go' zone around the part of the sculpture you are shaping. I tend to leave 10-20mm, about ½in, depending on the situation. Then if you do lose control of the saw the resulting damage is likely to be to this safety buffer, preserving the desired form.

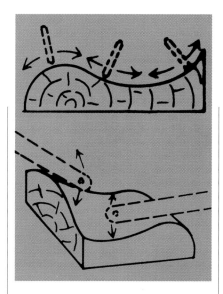

PARALLEL CUTS

It is possible to produce quite complex curves using only straight cuts with the chainsaw. Make parallel cuts about 20mm, ¾in apart, if possible across the grain. Then knock out the intervening pieces with a hammer or the back of an axe in free-splitting timbers, or use a mallet and gouge.

This is quite a safe technique, and can be combined with the floating technique described next to tidy up the admittedly rough surface produced. Again it is wise to leave a buffer zone to accommodate any errors you may make at this stage.

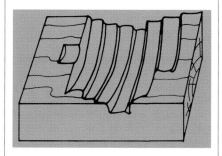

A series of parallel cuts with the intervening pieces knocked out

In very soft timbers I find I remove wood as shavings and sawdust rather than in pieces. I often cut slice after slice with the saw as described above, but leaving no intervening pieces to be knocked out later. Having the correct chain fitted makes this much easier: some chains are difficult to hold in position and tend to jump off the cut into the previous slot.

FLOATING

The technique I call floating consists of moving the bar from side to side across the surface, lightly enough to remove a thin layer of wood but not allowing the

Floating across a surface, the bar moving from side to side while the angle of the saw is adjusted to keep the bar perpendicular to the surface

saw to pause and cut in at any point. This is a useful technique for removing bark or sapwood, and for refining any surface that has already been roughly shaped.

Initially you will find it difficult to prevent the bar digging in and cutting, and perhaps ruining the surface. With practice, a light touch and fluid rocking of the bar from side to side will give good control. By varying the direction of attack you can make the surface true if required. Also, if you have cut an unintended slot, varying the direction of the cut will allow the chain to float over it and not drop in and deepen it.

With a sharp chain and a light

touch, a lot of timber can be shaped with this technique, especially on the outside of a piece. Complex curves can be accommodated, using the nose of the bar if necessary to enter hollows (see below). The finished surface can be true enough to move directly to sanding.

There is one important rule when floating: keep the bar at right angles to the surface being cut. This means the machine will need to be rotated with your wrists to follow the curves. Allowing the bar to lean over on the wood may result in it biting or bouncing, with resulting damage to the surface. Some chains are more forgiving than others in this regard.

Floating demands total concentration, and as it puts a lot of strain on your wrists it is best done in short bursts. It is not particularly dangerous, though if you are using the nose of the bar in a deep hollow do not allow the top quadrant of the nose to touch any overhang as this could cause kickback.

CUTTING CURVES

To cut curves the trick is to use the nose of the bar as much as possible. Hold the chainsaw above the level of the work so that only the rounded bar end comes in contact with the wood. Try drawing curves on the surface of the wood using the bar nose, starting at the point furthest from your body and drawing the saw towards you. You can make a controlled shallow cut which curves quite smoothly.

Move your whole body fluidly while maintaining a gentle but steady pressure on the bar. Keep the tip down so that most of the cutting is done on the curved end of the bar. It cuts fast because the chain passing over the curve offers more bite than on the flat side of the bar.

To cut more deeply and define the shape marked out by your original curved cut, repeat the cut moving the bar slightly away from the area you wish to preserve, and into the waste wood. Go deeper. Make further cuts, each time moving the bar slightly further into the waste wood and away from the original cut. If you don't widen the cut with the tip of the bar, the deeper cuts will start to erode the part you want to save.

You are cutting a curve with a straight, flat bar so there has to be some width for the bar to twist in. As the groove gets deeper the chain on the top of the nose may start to cut as well. At this point there could be a risk of kickback, but the movement towards you with constant steady pressure helps minimise this. Take special care though,

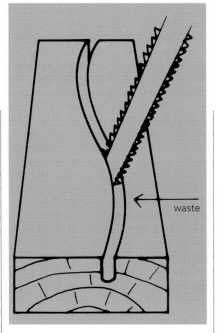

Cutting a deep curve with the tip of the bar, moving into the waste wood as the cut is widened on each stroke

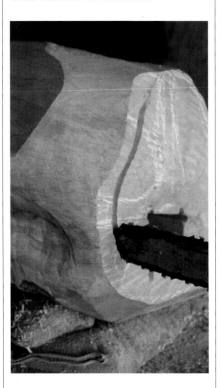

Above **The nose of the saw used to cut a curve. Subsequent cuts into the waste widen the cut**

Right **The cut is deepened and widened to allow the bar to twist within the hollow**

as you enter each cut, that the top of the nose does not contact the wood. Fluid sweeping movements are better than rigid over-controlled pressure.

With a powerful saw, this technique can be controlled, fluid and fast. In fact it comes close to being the equivalent for the sculptor of the free expression that painters such as Jackson Pollock experience as they trickle paint on the canvas.

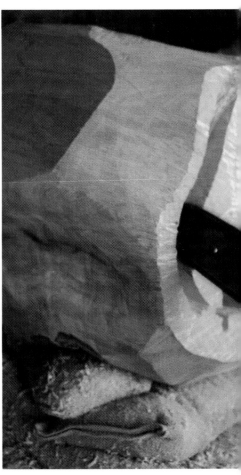

NIBBLING

When working within a hollow form or cavity, lack of space does not allow most of the previously described techniques to be performed properly. You need to expand the cavity gradually, using careful controlled cuts, so that the bar does not damage the surrounding work. Using this technique, the timber is all removed as chips or, as is often the case when working with the grain, as long thin ribbons.

The initial hollow must be large enough to accommodate the bar, at least in one direction. Such a cavity can be produced by nosing (described next) or with a drill and wood bits, using a gouge to remove the core. Often there will be little extra space, so control of the chainsaw is crucial.

Set the saw in motion first, then insert the bar into the cavity and make a cut towards what will eventually be its perimeter. If the work is arranged so that you are cutting downwards then gravity is working with you. Carefully raise the saw so as not to strike the top of the cavity, and make the next cut parallel to and immediately adjacent to the first.

With succeeding cuts a keyhole-shaped cavity is created. The key slot is expanded little by little, if possible turning the work from time to time so that you continue to cut downwards as you work. Ideally the bar should be at right angles to the developing perimeter, though this is not always feasible. With some chains the bar tends to jump off the cut, so having a suitable chain can make a great difference.

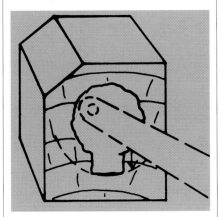

Nibbling to expand a cavity. Care must be taken to avoid kickback

This can be tense and demanding work, and also rather slow. Attention must be paid at all times to the position of the bar within the cavity so that the top of the nose is not allowed to strike the top of the cavity and cause kickback.

NOSING

Nosing, or boring, is a technique for creating very deep cavities or cutting holes through timber by pushing the nose of the bar straight into the wood. It is dangerous and hard on the saw, so I prefer not to use it. Some saw manufacturers apparently do not approve of it, though it is a widely used technique.

To start the cut, hold the saw with the nose down at an angle and cut a slot 10-20mm, about ½in deep. With the saw running in this slot, rotate the body of the saw so that the bar is now at right angles to the timber, maintaining steady firm pressure to force it deeper. If planning to cut right through the timber, know where the bar will emerge and plan your supports accordingly before commencing the cut.

Obviously the critical point is when the angle of the bar, including the top quadrant of the nose, will be in contact with the wood, and kickback is possible. Once the blade is deeper in the wood, control becomes easier. The initial slot should be deep enough to help hold the bar in position as it changes angle, and steady firm pressure is essential as the saw is rotated.

Needless to say, the timber should be very firmly supported when attempting this cut, which is not recommended for beginners. Using four such cuts arranged in a square, a section of wood can be removed to create a cavity, a technique often used in making post and rail fences.

SHAVING

Shaving is a useful technique for removing thin layers of timber from a surface with good control. It resembles

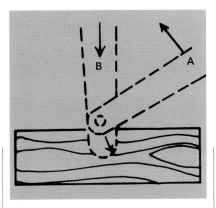

Nosing is not a technique for the beginner. At position 'A' the saw has created a slot ready for the whole saw to be rotated to the vertical position 'B' while maintaining firm downwards pressure to prevent kickback

floating except that the bar is not kept at 90° to the surface but instead lies flat. Generally it is more convenient to handle the saw with the blade vertical, so if possible turn the work so that the face to be shaved is also vertical.

The trick with shaving is to take only about half the thickness of the chain (the kerf) on each pass. If you take too much on any pass you will find that you are just sawing through the wood. By remaining on the surface the speed of cutting is greatly increased, control is easier, and the saw can follow around at least the broader curves. The surface produced can be so smooth that you can proceed directly to sanding.

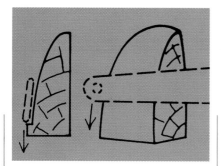

Shaving using the normal cutting edge of the bar. Less than the thickness of the chain is being removed at each pass

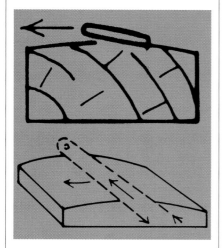

Shaving using the trailing edge of the bar, giving greater control of the depth of cut. Care must be taken to adjust to the saw's tendency to push towards the user

Normally the underside of the bar used for cutting is also used for shaving, but it is also possible to use the upper or trailing edge of the bar. Check the chain is not too slack on the bar first. Some caution is required as there will be a change in the forces operating, and the saw tends to push you away rather than pull you in to the cut. Again care is needed to ensure that the top quadrant of the nose does not dig in and cause kickback.

The bar itself lies flat on the surface being worked, and the saw slides across this surface, slightly angled so that it is the trailing edge that does the cutting. The effect is to limit the depth of cut to half the difference between the bar thickness and the cutter thickness, or kerf, a matter of only a millimetre or two.

Primal Event in progress: up to this stage, all shaping has been done with a chainsaw

The cutting is actually being done by the side of the cutting tooth. This is a most useful technique for the sculptor, but I suggest you experiment cautiously with it until experience gives you confidence.

IN SUMMARY

In practice, the eight techniques above are seldom so distinct when I am working. No doubt other people have developed different techniques, for the chainsaw is a versatile tool. The power of the saw, the hardness of the wood, and the type of chain fitted, will all affect the choice of technique. So too will simple laziness, for often it is more comfortable to continue plugging away with a technique that is working, however poorly, than to stop and realign the work or try out something new.

However, the techniques I describe do offer a range of options to expand the potential of your chainsaw so that it can be used safely and efficiently. ●

DON'T BE A BLOCKHEAD!

JOHN MIGNONE GIVES TIPS ON BLOCKING OUT AS HE CARVES A MAN'S HEAD

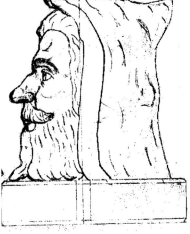

Although I started carving in the early 1980s I could not find the tools I thought I would need. Sharpening techniques also eluded me.

When I finally got started I floundered for two years, getting nowhere until I discovered people with art backgrounds did very well when they tried their hand at carving. I saw their first carvings were very good.

I realised carving was not so much the technical aspect of putting a tool to the wood as it was artistic vision and sight.

Then I came across a book entitled *Drawing on the Riqht Side of the Brain* by Betty Edwards. She reinforced what I had been thinking about: you need a certain perspective to carve well.

Drawing has helped develop this, and it has been essential since I enjoy carving faces and figures of people.

I have been told many of my busts have an English look to them. My work is a result of looking at pictures and carvings of people. I do not aim for a particular style, although I admit two of my favourite carvers are Ian Norbury and Ray Gonzalez, both from England.

For this project of a hooded man with a beard and moustache I drew a sketch of his front and side profiles. The bust, about half life size, was done from a block of basswood (*Tilia americana*) 180mm, 7in high x 145mm, 5¾in deep x 120mm, 4¾in wide.

I am most often asked about blocking out the basic features rather than refining them. This is why I will take the reader only so far on the face.

Though I show a finished bust and offer a front and side pattern, I would suggest dealing with such refinements as hair are subject to individual taste.

A beard, for example, can be rendered simply or very detailed. The same is true for the scalp hair, which I stylised to appear wavy with little if any detail.

....

Above **The finished bust.**
Left **The sketches of front and side profiles.**

PROFILES

Instead of using a bandsaw to establish the profiles in the wood I started by separating the face from the hood. The proportions were slightly larger than necessary to compensate for minor mistakes.

If you are carving a face you learn a lot more by starting off with a square block. What you learn is to block out the features in their correct positions. You cannot master this when you bandsaw the profiles.

The next step was drawing in a vertical centreline using a flexible ruler. This not only divided the face but also gave me an axis for the first part of the anatomy to be carved, the nose.

After drawing lines representing the top and bottom of the nose I began by cutting away wood from under it.

I recommend using a gouge instead of a knife. If you use a knife you end up with a sharp cut at the base of the nose. Faces are not like that. Instead there is a gentle curve where the nose blends into the upper lip. I used a 5mm, ³⁄₁₆in No 9 for the wood removal.

I then moved on to removing wood between the top of the nose and the brow line. Using a 35mm, 1³⁄₈in No 2 gouge I started just below the line representing the top of the nose, working the tool across the plane of the face.

This is a large gouge for a small carving, but the larger the gouge the easier it is to remove wood. I do not waste time with small tools to hog off material.

I next worked on rounding the forehead into the sides of the face. If this figure did not have a beard I would have continued working down, rounding the chin at the same time.

This is part of a process that has me rounding the wood as often as possible. By doing this I am getting the features as close to where they should be as I can. I used a large fishtail, a 25mm, 1in No 5.

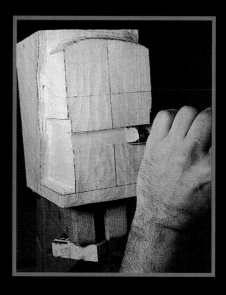

Blocking out the nose after a vertical centreline has been established and horizontal lines are drawn for the top and bottom of the nose.

Establishing the brow and nose profile.

Removing wood from the sides of the nose.

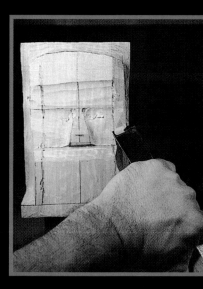

A human face is approximately four eye widths wide at the eye plane. Lines are drawn to represent the limits of that plane and where the face curves around to the sides of the head.

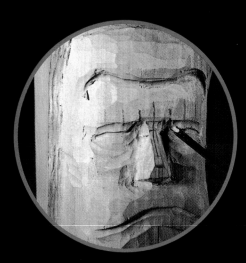

Creating a drooping piece of flesh that will give the face some age.

Giving emphasis to the cheek bones.

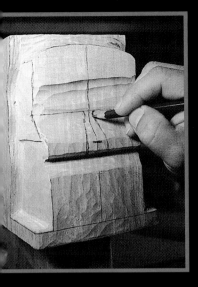

ating the sides of the nose.

Creating the indentations on the sides of the nose requires pushing a gouge straight into the wood.

wering the area below the moustache.

Establishing the width of the eyes.

aping the eye sockets.

Creating the lower lids by pushing a gouge straight into the wood.

EYE SOCKETS

I then chose an 18mm, ²³⁄₃₂in No 8 gouge to cut in where the eye sockets curve into the sides of the head. This attention to detail is something I see missing in many facial carvings. The eye socket areas are left too flat when in fact they curve around the head.

I used the same gouge to remove some wood above the brow line and deepen the top of the nose. I left extra wood for the hair that protruded from under the hood, knowing I could go back later and take more away.

I next needed to establish the sides of the nose. Taking a 10mm, ⅜in No 9 gouge and placing it at the bottom of the brow and top of the nose, I pushed it into the wood as far as it would go by hand. This created the indentations on either side of the nose.

I then used the 18mm, ²³⁄₃₂in No 8 gouge to remove wood on each side of the nose. Taking wood away from the base of the nose where it meets the lip is not as difficult as removing wood where the nose meets the brow.

When I got to the indentations which have to blend into the eye sockets, I had to make a slicing or skewing action to get a smooth cut.

The sides of the nose blend into the cheeks, leaving no sharp line or crease. Also be aware there is a muscle that extends from the top of the nose to the sides of the mouth. It follows the shape of a gentle curve.

HUMAN FACE

Besides making a nose too sharp looking, another common mistake I see is with the profile of the nose.

Nearly half a human nose is behind the upper lip. The mistake carvers make is in placing the nose so too much is sticking out from the face.

But because of the moustache on this bust, the tip of the nose will extend only a fraction beyond the front of the moustache.

I have read that as a rule of thumb

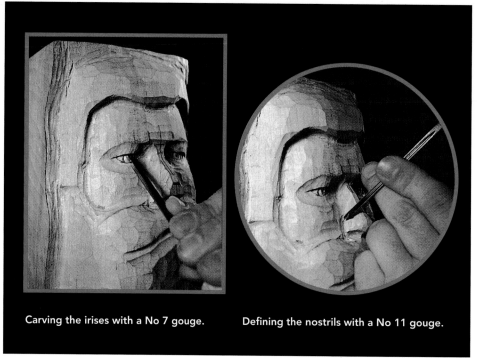

Carving the irises with a No 7 gouge.

Defining the nostrils with a No 11 gouge.

Photos by Roger Schroeder.

exposed eyeball. But it is not totally exposed because the upper and lower lids cover part of it.

If you were to show the entire iris the expression would appear shocked or frightened, not a look you want your bust to have.

I took a 6mm, ¼in No 7 gouge and cut in the shape of each iris, popping out thin slivers of wood in the process. Blocking out continued with more work on the nose. I flattened the bridge of the nose slightly using a 10mm, ⅜in No 5 gouge. I held the gouge bevel up to make a convex cut.

I further outlined the nostrils using a 10mm, ⅜in No 8 for the tops of the nostrils.

For the final shaping of the nostril crease I used a 2mm, 3⁄32in No 11 gouge and outlined the area. ●

Drawing on the Right Side of the Brain by Betty Edwards, Perigee Books, published by The Putnam Publishing Group, 200 Madison Avenue, New York, NY 10016, USA. Price $13.95

John Mignone, 48, is a professional woodcarver, a classical musician and tree propagator who resides in East Meadow, Long Island, New York, USA. He and his father have been hardwood growers and propagators for 35 years. He has been carving professionally since 1990.

the human face is five eye widths across. I ran into a problem with that rule because my heads ending up looking too wide.

I now make the face four eye widths across the eye plane, which includes the sockets. Beyond the sockets the skull gradually enlarges to a fifth eye width at the area of the ears, but not including them.

Once I established the width of the face by making vertical lines on the wood, I cut back from those lines, removing wood and rounding the face. I used a 25mm, 1in No 2 fishtail gouge.

I did more work rounding the cheeks, shaping the nose, establishing the moustache and the hair line.

Making the nostrils takes some care because they have a deep crease as they merge with the face.

Instead of using a knife or V tool I took a 6mm, ¼in No 9 gouge and blocked out the nostrils. This created a softer look than another tool would have made.

Next I cut away some of the moustache to reveal more of the nose. I also cut in a line below the moustache to establish where it rested above the upper lip.

A common mistake that can surface later is to make the lower lip too far forward, giving the face a bulldog appearance. Make sure the lower lip is set farther back.

Next I went to work on the eye sockets. I drew pencil lines for the width of each eye as well as a centreline, and carved away wood from where the tops of the eye sockets were located.

I wanted this figure to appear nearing the end of middle age. To create this look I needed to make a piece of skin that drooped down and covered the top eyelid.

Using a 5mm, ³⁄₁₆in No 9 gouge, I made an S-shaped cut to represent this drooping skin. Since the skin overlapped the top eyelid, I had to lower the wood under it while keeping in mind a round eyeball was there. Another mistake carvers make is flattening the eyeballs.

EYEBALLS

After lowering the eyeball area with a 25mm, 1in No 5 fishtail gouge I needed to deepen the cheekbones. I took a 15mm, ⅝in No 8 gouge and removed wood from the sides of the head toward the nose. I also worked on the brow, putting more curvature into it.

I next went to work on the eyeballs. After using a 10mm, ⅜in No 8 gouge to deepen the areas next to the nose, I made a cut under the eyeballs using a 10mm, ⅜in No 9 gouge.

I then used a 10mm, ⅜in No 5 gouge and made a straight-in cut to form the bottom eyelids. To further separate the eyelids, I used a sharp knife and pared away slivers of wood. While doing this I was conscious of maintaining the roundness of the eyeball.

An iris takes up about half the

SHADOWLANDS

IN THE FIRST OF TWO ARTICLES, GRAHAM BULL STUDIES THE EFFECT OF LIGHT AND SHADE, AND HIGHLIGHTS THE IMPORTANCE OF SHADOW TO THE CARVER

The importance of shadow for the woodcarver can never be over-stated. Like most artistic skills, its effective use can be developed only by constant experimentation.

The easiest way to understand just how important shadow is, is to consider that whereas a painter has an infinite range of colours the woodcarver has only two, the colour of wood itself, and the dark of the shadow that can be carved into it.

True, shadows can be developed to reflect different degrees of darkness, but essentially we are dealing with one colour.

I will concentrate on relief carving, as it is here the concept of shadow creation is more easily understood.

If we strip the whole subject down to its bare elements, as unemotionally and analytically as possible, the only reason we carve wood is to decorate an otherwise boring surface. Before you accuse me of blasphemy, consider the statement from the position of the observer, not the carver.

To the non-woodie a piece of wood is just that, a piece of wood. A piece of wood becomes a beautiful carving only once we have covered it with a pleasing arrangement of shadows. You can see the carved design only by virtue of the shadows that compose it.

PHOTOGRAPHY

Photographers know shadow. It can enhance the natural colours in the picture, or interfere with them. Black and white photography in particular, trains the brain to interpret in black and white what the eye sees in colour, as an image made up of varying shades of grey.

This is the crux of the whole matter. To successfully develop shadow, you must start to see things differently, so from now on when you think relief carving, think shadow.

Every time you make a cut, ask yourself what kind of shadow it will make. Or better still, before you make a cut decide what shadow you want to make.

It is extremely important to consider the light you are carving by. If you don't use the right source, it will be impossible to see whether you are creating the right shadows or not.

The two most common forms of lighting are the fluorescent tube and the light bulb. Each is designed for a specific purpose:

The fluorescent tube is designed to produce lots of light in an economical form. It is for use in places where cheap, non directional and shadowless light is needed, places like offices and factories.

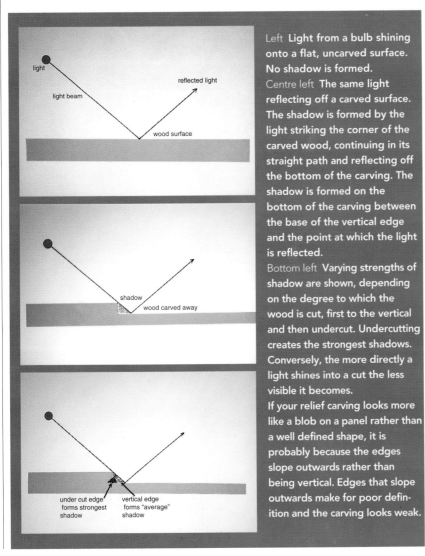

Left Light from a bulb shining onto a flat, uncarved surface. No shadow is formed.

Centre left The same light reflecting off a carved surface. The shadow is formed by the light striking the corner of the carved wood, continuing in its straight path and reflecting off the bottom of the carving. The shadow is formed on the bottom of the carving between the base of the vertical edge and the point at which the light is reflected.

Bottom left Varying strengths of shadow are shown, depending on the degree to which the wood is cut, first to the vertical and then undercut. Undercutting creates the strongest shadows. Conversely, the more directly a light shines into a cut the less visible it becomes.

If your relief carving looks more like a blob on a panel rather than a well defined shape, it is probably because the edges slope outwards rather than being vertical. Edges that slope outwards make for poor definition and the carving looks weak.

Top right **A relief pattern directly below a fluorescent tube. Note the poorly defined nature of the pattern.**

Centre right **The same pattern placed directly under an unshaded light bulb. Direct light from a filament tends to concentrate the light in a far more coherent fashion. Even the colours are truer.**

Bottom right **If the bare bulb is shaded to concentrate the light, and is moved to one side of the carving (in this case to the left), the density of the shadows increases, enhancing the visibility of features still further. The arrowed error is not visible in the first picture.**

Fluorescent light is deliberately diffuse, it doesn't throw shadows. It is therefore inappropriate for woodcarving or any activity, including woodturning and general woodwork, where you need to see everything you are creating, especially the mistakes!

If you have set up your workshop using fluorescent lighting, then my advice is to remove it, or at least don't use it for woodwork.

Strong cross lighting is better for woodcarving than overhead fluorescent lighting.

If you use fluorescent lighting and think you have done a wonderful job until you take your carving out into direct sunlight, where you suddenly see all sorts of mess, this is the reason. Natural direct sunlight creates shadow forming cross-lighting and that reveals all.

In fact in Sydney, Australia for example, the best lighting of all is the low sunlight of autumn, winter and spring mornings and afternoons when the deepest shadows are cast. In summer in the middle part of the day the sun is very much overhead, creating little cross lighting. If only we could stop the world going round!

EXPERIMENT

As we start to experiment with this shadow theory, we will discover the

way we can use different shadows for effect, right to the point where we start to create illusions with shadow, and make things look as they are not.

We will learn to tell lies with shadows and create all sorts of illusions such as depth where there is almost none, and the impression of curved surfaces that are really almost flat.

These things are very useful where you want to create decorative wall panels with timber only an inch or so thick, or the roundness of lily leaves on the flat of a chair back.

The more developed the up-front planning of our carvings, the more likely we will be to get good results for our efforts.

So for example, if we are to carve a surround for the fireplace in the lounge room, we should consider the kind of lighting that will be in use when the fire is being used. Is it a bulb in the ceiling, or a standard lamp off to one side, or both?

If we are carving a chair back in the kitchen, will the kitchen be in use during the day when the predominant light is through a window, or at night with an overhead fluorescent tube? Will a pediment on top of a wall cupboard be lit from above or from the bottom up?

A good way to assess lighting requirements is simply to move the carving from one room to another and note the changes in its appearance.

Once the lighting is sorted out, we can plan the overall carving. For example, if we are to carve a music stand to be used for on-stage performance, where the predominant lighting could be left, right, top or bottom of stage, or any combination of the whole lot at once, what better design for classical performances than the Byzantine rosette shown in the photograph?

No matter where the light is coming from, this pierced relief design will always show a multitude of shadow activity.

SURFACES

The planning process asks questions such as: Do I make a surface (such as the surfaces on the vines in the rosette) convex or concave? A convex surface will create one block of shadow when light falls across it, whereas a concavity will create two blocks of shadow across its surface.

If you want shadows dancing all over, then in this example go concave, as with the rosette.

Apart from the considerations of practicality, availability and workability of timber, the colour of the wood should be considered. Shadows are more easily seen on lighter wood than darker.

Avoid carving elaborate shadow detail on dark wood, and if you stain light wood dark, much of your hard work will disappear.

The light coloured oak (*Quercus spp*) carving from St Andrew's Cathedral at Inverness in Scotland has sufficient shadows created by carving against the light background to make the small figures easily visible. This photograph was taken with the available light at the time.

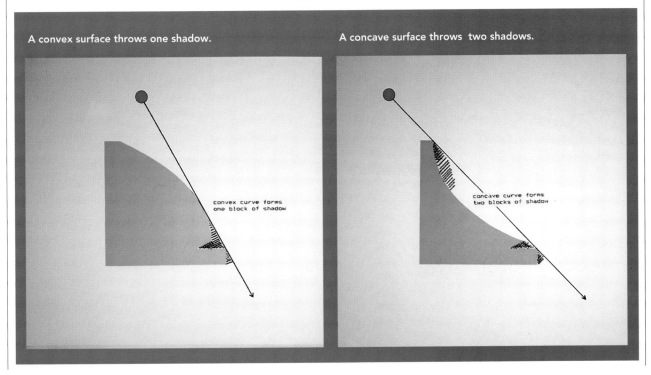

A convex surface throws one shadow.

A concave surface throws two shadows.

convex curve forms one block of shadow

concave curve forms two blocks of shadow

Right **A carved panel from St Andrew's Cathedral, Inverness, Scotland.**
Below **A darker carving from St Andrew's Cathedral, Sydney, Australia.**

A darker carved panel from St Andrew's Cathedral in Sydney, Australia, has less natural light, and the design carved in dark stained timber is really only visible in artificial light.

In this case, a spotlight was placed in such a way as to create a high shine on the high, flatter surfaces so they contrast to the darkness of the deeper curved surfaces, which reflect the same light at different angles so they appear dull. The detail of the carving is easily seen only by placing it in an 'unnatural' state.

Decor is also a consideration, so you cannot say one cathedral's carvings are better than the other. Nevertheless, these two examples show how the colour of the wood can make an enormous difference to a carving's visibility.

In the next article I will show how to create illusion with shadow, including depth and perspective. ●

Graham Bull is proprietor of the Whistlewood Studio and Craft Barn in Sydney, Australia. Self-taught, he has been a woodcarver for some 34 years and teaches carving in all its forms to about 100 people each year, from schoolchildren and hobbyists to professional woodworkers

SHADOWLANDS

PART TWO GRAHAM BULL CONCLUDES HIS WALK ON THE DARK SIDE OF CARVING TECHNIQUE

In the previous article I looked at some of the basic principles surrounding the subject of shadows. As you begin to develop these basic concepts, one of the most intriguing aspects of shadow work will begin to emerge, its ability to play tricks on the eye.

Carving a shadow line around a pattern separates it from the background. The stronger the shadow, the greater the appearance of depth

It is simply a matter of realising that the more we experiment, the more we can come up with. Sometimes if we want something to look like a particular thing, we need to carve it in exactly the opposite way to the true image.

How do we work out what to put where? It is all very well to say experiment, but there is a limit to how much time is available to do such things. Here are some hints and tips to add to your collection. You will be amazed at what you can get away with!

- A shadow line around the perimeter of a design will separate it from the background, increase visual intensity and apparent depth.
- A concave item set against a flat background will create a significant contrast and make it more obvious. A convex curve will do the opposite.
- A shadow line strategically placed in a carving will delineate one part from another, highlighting changes in angles, making them appear greater than is in fact the case.
- A little bit goes a long way. A small variation in the curvature of a surface will be interpreted and if necessary translated by the brain to conform to the memory perception of the item in real life. In other words, the brain will often fill in the blanks and see what the carver intended, even if it isn't real. This is particularly effective to the untrained eye of the casual observer.
- A flat surface will be very obvious in a carving of curves, because the surface will reflect light in a totally different direction from that of the surfaces surrounding it, and will tend not to cast shadows. So unless you want a surface to be very obvious, put a curve on it.

Remember, in nature there are no flat surfaces except in such things as crystals, so unless you want flat surfaces for effect, get rid of them. This applies especially to carving in the round.

PERSPECTIVE

The phenomenon of perspective is as fascinating and perplexing a topic as shadow, and as much fun to come to grips with.

There are many texts on the subject of perspective, particularly in art, technical drawing and architecture. But these are essentially pen on paper activities, using lines to make the perspective work. Woodcarving however, has to draw lines with shadows, so no shadow, no perspective!

By playing around with the infinite combinations of shape and shadow, you can create an infinite variety of perceived shapes. In fact perception is the crux of the matter.

This foliage pattern shows the effect of shadow quite clearly.
a) The opening V tool cut.
b) The first gouge incision away from the outline of the pattern.
c) The outward sloping edge, casting virtually no shadow.
d) The shadow caused by the vertical edge.
e) The stronger shadow caused by undercutting.
The actual depth of the incision at d is identical to the depth at e (3mm, ⅛in), although e looks deeper. Shadow creates the illusion of depth.

Above left **If shadow can be used to create the illusion of distance, then can it also be used to change the shape of things?**
In the photograph the curl of this leaf looks round. The roundness of the curl is created by placing a strong shadow beneath it, that is under the edges, then by carving a strong elliptical curve along one edge and trailing the other edge away just enough to change the direction of the reflected light, while throwing a very faint, graduated shadow over the sloping surface.
You are not conscious of this graduated surface shadow, but it creates the illusion the curve is much greater than it really is.

Left **A cross section of the leaf, highlighting the different curves and the undercuts around the edges. The curl in the leaf is created by carving a strong curve on one edge and placing a shadow under the other, which can also give it greater apparent depth.**

Left **Knave of Spades, a large carved panel adapted from a printed Swiss Alchemist's playing card series of the 17th century. In particular look at the village pump-stand on the left hand side.**
Right **A cross-section of the pump-stand carving. A combination of shadow lines and shadows over curved surfaces creates an illusion of depth and shape.**

undercut

concave surface

surface slopes
inwards

cross section of
village pump stand

What we perceive pleases or displeases us. If we like the look of what we see, we are happy with it. If we don't we aren't. So whatever you do, if you create a pleasurable perception, you have succeeded in your endeavours.

Do not mistake perception for perfection, as often the more perfect the detail the less pleasurable the perception.

Remember the brain is able to, and will always interpret things, the way it wants them to be. It will fill in details that are not there, and will make up or alter shapes and perspectives to suit the overall images it expects to see.

If a certain shadow makes a carving look better, keep it, and try to work out why. The chances are that more shadows will make it look better still. ●

Graham Bull is proprietor of the Whistlewood Studio and Craft Barn in Sydney, Australia. Self-taught, he has been a woodcarver for some 34 years and teaches carving in all its forms to about 100 people each year, from schoolchildren and hobbyists to professional woodworkers

Above **Perspective:**
Terrace Lounge Room carved by Andrew Tarlinton, Sydney, Australia.

The dimensions of the carving are 350 x 300mm, 14 x 12in, and the depth is 12mm, ½in, in jelutong (*Dyera costulata*).

You automatically see the carving as a whole, which is the first secret to its success. It looks like the lounge room in a terrace. Whatever its inherent weaknesses as a carving, your brain accepts the subject for what it purports to be and in the first instance, glosses over any imperfections.

The overall depth of the lounge is 14mm, ⁹⁄₃₂in, although it looks significantly greater. Given normal ratios, if the length of the lounge is about 150mm, 6in, the depth of the carved lounge chair should be about 60mm, 2⅜in. Yet it is squashed into a depth about one sixth of that. Shadow has been used to change the perspective.

This is clear if you look at the arms of the chair. They are angled inwards so the back looks narrower than the front. The exaggerated angle of the arms increases the perception of distance and adds to the apparent depth of the chair.

To the brain the back of the chair appears further away. The use of shadow work around the cushions, underneath the chair and around the arms helps to create the illusion of depth.

The stairs demonstrate a different distortion of reality, giving the impression of a flight leading upwards. The first stair slopes at about 45°, the second at roughly 30°. Each step is undercut around its edges, creating shadow lines that distinguish each from the next.

The spiral effect is created by making each successive, wedge-shaped step narrower and more horizontal than the preceding one, so that each reflects light differently and the whole appears to recede upwards. The dark shadow on the third step gives the illusion of depth and makes it look longer than it really is, when it is actually less than half the length of the first step.

The wall with the curtains is similarly carved in perspective, with the skirting board and cornice converging on one another in the distance (which is 14mm, ⁹⁄₃₂in, in the carving).

The ceiling is carved at an angle that is all but vertical, that slopes just enough to throw a shadow over it to make it look flat. The important thing is that it is at a different angle from the walls, so it reflects light differently.

DIVIDE AND RULE

JIM COOPER SHOWS HOW TO MAKE A PAIR OF PROPORTIONAL DIVIDERS FOR SIZING UP A CARVING FROM A MAQUETTE

Many carvers like to work from a maquette (clay model of the finished piece), but it is not always feasible to make a full size one, especially if you are doing a large carving.

Making a small maquette will still be helpful in visualising the work, and will also give the opportunity to experiment with different shapes and positions to refine the design.

But there is the problem of how to use the small model to give accurate dimensions for the finished piece. You need a process to take information from the maquette to the workpiece, because it is difficult to do this well purely by eye, though of course working by eye will be a major part of the operation.

Even experienced carvers use a lot of information from the maquette. The creative work, or art, has gone into

making it, and then a little science is needed to speed up the rest of the work.

Measurements can be taken with a tape or rule, but dividers are much more convenient. Each measurement will have to be multiplied by the enlargement ratio, which gets difficult if you are not using whole numbers. Using a pair of proportional dividers makes the whole job easier.

DIVIDERS

Dividers consist of two arms, both having points at each end. If the arms are pivoted as in a pair of scissors, the ratio of the gap at one end to that at the other will always be the same. The ratio will depend on where you put the pivot.

If you put the pivot in the centre points of both arms, the gaps at both ends will be the same. There is a ratio of

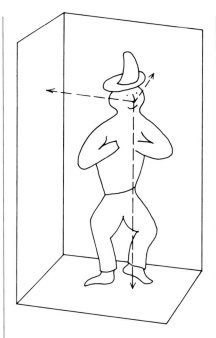

Finding a fixed reference point would require putting the maquette and workpiece in a corner and measuring three dimensions

one to one, shown as 1:1. If the arms are pivoted at one third along their lengths, the gap at one end will be twice the size of the smaller gap, a ratio of 2:1. This ratio will remain constant however wide apart you spread the arms.

You can buy dividers with a movable pivot point which can be locked anywhere along their length. Whole number ratio settings are marked and there is a guide pin which locates these for greater accuracy.

My metal dividers are 12in, 305mm long which means they are only suitable for small work, but you can make larger, less sophisticated wooden dividers quite easily.

The drawing shows the dimensions for various ratio settings, but these are not vital as for most carvers a constant setting is what is needed, rather than an exact whole number setting. Remember, though, if your instrument is not exact, do not mix measurement taking with another instrument.

I made another large set of

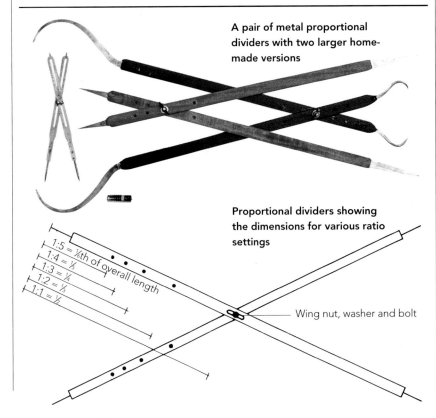

A pair of metal proportional dividers with two larger home-made versions

Proportional dividers showing the dimensions for various ratio settings

1:5 = ⅙th of overall length
1:4 = ⅕
1:3 = ¼
1:2 = ⅓
1:1 = ½

Wing nut, washer and bolt

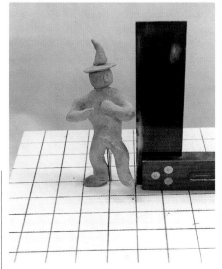

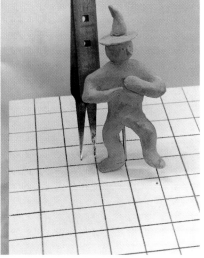

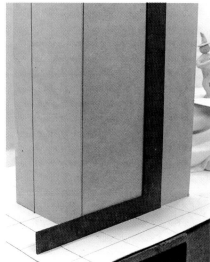

Extreme parts of the maquette are found with a square and marked on the base grid

Dimensions are taken from the grid and reference point with the small end of the dividers before being transferred to the large grid with the other end of the dividers

Above **The carving block is placed on the reference points on the large grid and vertical lines drawn with a square**
Below **Vertical measurements are taken and marked on the block using the dividers**

dividers using the ends of an old set of calliper dividers. If using curved ends like these, it is important to ensure the points are on the same centre line as the centre of the pivot.

MEASURING

To fix a point you will need three dimensions, one vertical and two horizontal, but you can only take these if you have somewhere from which to measure.

You could put the maquette in a corner which would give two walls and a floor from which to measure, but the workpiece would also need to be in a corner and the right distance away

An easier way is to use fixed reference points on a floor grid

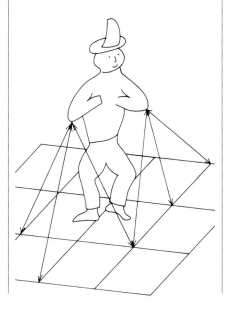

from the walls for it to work. In practice this would be difficult.

You can, however, take the vertical dimensions from the floor, a fixed plane, and the floor can also be used when taking measurements from fixed points by using a base grid and a square.

This method will give several critical points in the early stages of a carving, but as work progresses other methods must be found for finding dimensions of other points on the carving.

I have used a simple figure maquette as an example which I enlarged three times. Remember when enlarging, any errors will be multiplied by the same ratio, so it is important to be accurate.

First I drew a base grid and stood my modelling clay figure on it. I put location marks on the maquette so it could be accurately relocated in case it moved.

Then I used a square to locate three extreme points on the figure, the elbows and left foot, and mark them on the base.

I then drew a grid three times larger, using the proportional dividers to step off the grid, and put reference letters and numbers on the lines to match those on the smaller grid.

Using the small end of the dividers, I took the dimension from one point to a line on the small grid, then reversed the dividers and marked off the position on the large grid with the large end.

Each point had to be found by working from two grid lines at right angles to each other.

CARVING BLOCK

The next step was to locate the carving block on the marked extremity points on the large grid and draw vertical lines up the block from these points with a large square. The grid lines were also drawn up the block.

It was then possible to take vertical measurements with the dividers. First I marked the overall height, then one elbow and other key points. Note the points of the dividers must be kept in a vertical line.

I marked several positions to get the dimensions for the rim of the hat. When enough points had been marked I could join them up and remove waste areas.

As work continued it was necessary to keep checking back to the maquette in the same way. Calliper dividers were useful for checking dimensions across various parts of the figure and then adjustments could be made to the carving. Each time it was simply a case

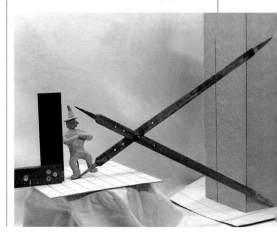

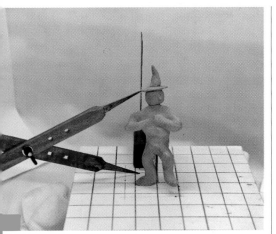

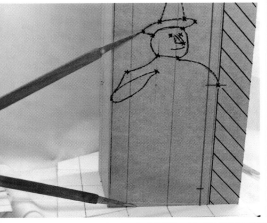

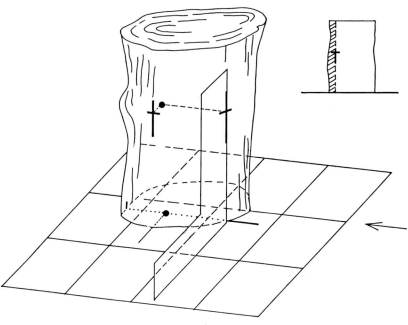

Above **Marking reference points on an irregular block. Extend lines away from the fixed reference points until a vertical line can be drawn with a square**

of reversing the proportional dividers to find the right enlarged dimension.

This method is fine if the blank is square and true, but the larger the work the less likely this is. You may even want to use a built up or laminated piece to give sufficient size without waste.

IRREGULAR SHAPES

When working on irregular shaped blocks the method is the same, but it becomes more difficult to apply. It then becomes a case of marking each point and cutting a little at a time as you go.

You may also have to extend lines away from critical points on the large grid until you can extend the lines vertically. Place the square on the grid where the extended line meets the edge of the block and mark the vertical in the area of the point. Then mark the height as described earlier. Waste can then be removed.

Even if you do not want to use the grid method for the transfer of dimensions, I am sure a set of proportional

dividers will be a worthwhile addition to your carving toolkit. They will also be useful for other jobs, such as enlarging a drawing, or even for picking up items that fall down the back of the workbench! ●

Jim Cooper, 51, has a degree in building and worked as a building and shopfitting manager. He started woodwork as a hobby in 1968 and has tried instrument making, turning and carving. He took up turning for a living during redundancy in the early 1980s, and in 1993 took a course in carpentry for historic building restoration. This led to restoration carving work, and he is also a part time college lecturer in carpentry and joinery.
A member of the BWA (Warwickshire region), Jim can be contacted for carving and turning commissions at 45 Bagnell Road, Kings Heath, Birmingham B13 0SJ.

ROUGH AND READY

WILLIAM GRAHAM EXPLAINS HOW A COPY CARVING MACHINE SAVES TIME AND HELPS HIS BUSINESS MAKE A PROFIT

Moneyreagh is a small village in Co. Down set among the rolling Castlereagh Hills. I have had my business here for 20 years. I learned woodcarving as a boy from an old wood and stone carver, who had worked for many years in London restoring the blitzed churches. Over the years, I have supplied many carved pieces for churches and public buildings.

I now find most of our work is for pubs and clubs around the province. Carving for fun is nice, but as a money making business it is difficult. People do not appreciate the time you spend on producing even the simplest item.

This is where the carving machine comes in. It almost eliminates the initial roughing out and sizing process, leaving you with the more pleasant finishing off.

For instance, all carvers find problems in getting the eyes and ears in the proper position and everything in proportion, or with multiple work, in achieving identical items.

I bought my machine some years ago. It is a four head Italian Bulleri, producing four exact clones from a single master, either in the round or flat.

SPEEDY SQUIRRELS

The procedure is extremely quick. For instance, I take a squirrel as the master and glue blocks of 3in, 75mm dried chestnut (*Aesculus hippocastanum*) together. This is left overnight to

....

The copy machine carves three squirrels simultaneously

harden. Any timber will do, some being better for different objects.

I tend to use lime (*Tilia vulgaris*) for finely detailed pieces, but we also buy many home grown supplies of sycamore (*Acer pseudoplatanus*), maple (*Acer campestre*), walnut (*Juglans regia*), beech (*Fagus sylvatica*), and cherry (*Prunus avium*).

The blocks, either two or four, depending on size, are loaded between centres on the lathe-type chucks. These revolve in either direction to offer up each face as required. We start with the largest cutter and go down in stages. The cutters work at a fast pace and soon the floor gets carpeted in chippings.

It is satisfying to see the objects take shape, as if by magic, and quite soon we can remove them from the machine for final finishing by hand.

CARVING TECHNIQUE

When the blank comes off the machine the full shape is there. All the major details are obvious such as eyes, fingers, toes and so on. The surface is sometimes woolly but this is reasonable for representing hair on animal figures.

We start by gouging in the main characteristics of the object. The big appealing eyes are carefully carved by removing the top layer of woolly timber, exposing the smooth surface below.

The lines around the eyes can be carved either with a parting or V tool or two opposing stabs with a slow gouge. Parting tools are difficult to sharpen and unless very sharp can cause serious damage. The fingers and toes are next, using the same technique of two opposing cuts with a small slow gouge.

We quickly remove the woolly surface and replace it with irregular tool marks to represent the animal's fur. This can be made more life-like by adding hair-like marks with a parting tool or the type of pyrography wire used with great success by decoy duck carvers.

By following this procedure we condense much of the work and can produce a presentable woodcarving in

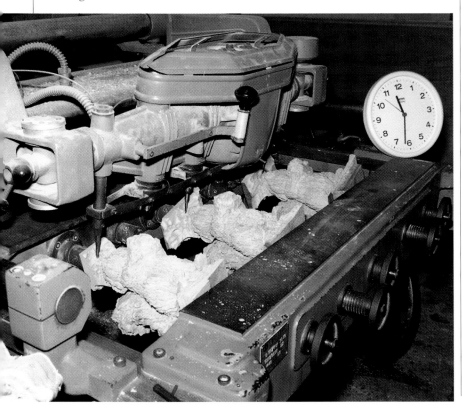

Top **Some of the carvings produced by the copy machine after finishing by hand**
Above **Coat of arms carved by Philip Steele for Limavady Council Chambers**

a short space of time. Most of these roughed out blocks are sold to woodcarvers so they can finish them, as we could not finish all we produce.

ENCOURAGING ENTERPRISE

One of our customers manufactures fine walking sticks with silver mounts. These are sold to collectors around the world and to stores like Harrods in London. We hand carve animal heads for some of his pieces.

Our carving business was set up with the help of L.E.D.U, a local enterprise agency helping small businesses to get established. The work we do is

done in a big way in Europe where factories turn out roughed out carvings by the million.

Whole districts are turned into woodcarving centres with schools for carvers and all kind of small businesses finishing carvings for sale. With the tourist boom, I think there is room for the carver in Britain and wonder why so many wooden items are imported.

Someone carving for pleasure can take a lot of time putting their own skill to good effect, giving the piece their individuality and personality, so no two pieces look exactly the same.

There are those, like myself, who are slaves to father time and must decide how long can be expended on a carving to give a reasonable profit. I have rarely seen any carving book or article give any indication of the time spent on a piece of work. Of course this varies considerably depending on the level of skill and range of tools.

In our workshop we are faced with the old problem of making the job pay. If you consider the cost of materials, laminating blocks, overheads, wages and so on, carving becomes like any other commercial enterprise, figures on a balance sheet.

With time and training, surprising speed can be achieved by a skilled man and quite intricate pieces leave our workshop in reasonable time. A coat of arms carved in walnut, for instance, was completed by Philip Steele (once my apprentice and one of the best carvers around) in 50 hours.

The purists say the use of carving machines is cheating, but I don't see it that way. In early times joiners roamed the forests looking for a tree or branch growing in a certain shape to ease their burden of laboriously cutting the timber to shape.

Carving machines of various kinds have been in use for a long time, removing the initial waste wood and leaving the carver to show their skill. Why not try it yourself, you may get a pleasant surprise. ●

Top **The different stages in carving a squirrel on the Bulleri copying machine**
Above **Operating the copy carving machine**

William Graham began his career in wood with jewellery boxes for his sisters when aged eight. After serving as a joiner in a shipbuilding firm, he was taught by a carver who had worked on the rebuilding of London churches destroyed in the Second World War. After working as a joiner and carver in Belfast he built his own workshop 20 years ago and now specialises in carvings and shop fitting work.

You can contact Grace Joinery Works at 30 Ballykeel Road, Moneyreagh, Co. Down BT23 6BN
Tel: 01232 448281

Timber supplied by
Hasletts,
Fivemiletown, Co.Tyrone
and McGregor and Son,
Sydenham Road, Belfast

Carving Tools supplied by
McMaster Tools, Church Street, Belfast

ALLY OF THE DOLLS

AURIEL MIMS DISCUSSES THE INSPIRATION AND TECHNIQUES BEHIND HER NORFOLK DOLLS

I was rather taken aback when approached by *Woodcarving* magazine, in fact I blushed on the other end of the phone. I had been found out as a fraud.

With no professional training as a woodcarver, never even having seen a real woodcarver at work, and having found no better tool than my beloved Stanley knife with which to finish my work, how could I possibly write an article for professional woodcarvers?

However, I was assured readers covered a wide range of skill and experience and my unorthodox methods might be of interest to them, and perhaps provide a good laugh?

For my part I realised I had a unique chance to glean ideas and advice from the real McCoy. I would be a fool to turn down such an opportunity, so here goes.

I made my first carved wooden doll for our first child, Flora, when she was five. My husband and I were living in the wilds of Norfolk making a precarious living from our wooden toys which we sold weekly on Norwich market.

The doll which was admired by various friends, led to my making similar dolls, sometimes portrait dolls, and over 15 years a design developed.

Some of my dolls have found homes in the USA, Canada, Sweden, Switzerland, Japan and Egypt. I sometimes wonder what they can see from their windowsill or shelf, I would love to know.

....

Woodcarving is a major feature in the personality of each doll.

COMPONENTS

The carved wooden components: heads, hands, lower leg and feet, are painted and finished in beeswax. These are drilled and stitched to a soft cloth body and dressed in natural fabrics.

The principle of such a design is probably inspired by the Parisian dolls of the 19th century, whose porcelain head and shoulders, lower arm and hands, and lower legs were stitched onto a kid body, stuffed with sawdust. The adaptation to a soft cloth body and wood components is simple and obvious.

Without the complication of jointed limbs, the doll has much less chance of being broken, or of hurting a child, but can still mimic most natural poses.

It was coming across local Edwardian photos which inspired the launching of my Norfolk Dolls three years ago. The open innocence of the faces of the children in those photos fascinated me, and it is this quality

Left **Carving a face. The cloth in the chops protects the wood from the vice.**
Centre left **...better than one.**
Below left **Carving the hands.**

which I try to capture in my dolls, each of which is different.

My aim initially was to establish Norfolk Dolls as a name, by concentrating on the children. Adult characters would be added later, dolls representing the Edwardian village community, such as the blacksmith, joiner, shopkeeper, vicar and schoolteacher.

These characters I am starting to work on now, but these photographs illustrate the process of making my Norfolk Doll children.

The process starts with drawings inspired by old photographs. Sometimes I use clay if I have difficulty in moving from the photo to three dimensions.

When I have the right face I draw the head to scale (the dolls stand at 450–600mm, 18–20in tall), and cut a profile in paper which I draw onto a block of lime (*Tilia vulgaris*).

Boots, legs and hands are also marked out on lime, and are cut on a bandsaw, together with the head. Boys' hands are larger than girls' hands, and boots are different too. It is surprising how much character can be expressed in a boot.

Then comes the vice, chisel and mallet. I use a range of chisels and gouges, starting with the largest. There is something very satisfying about the hard physical work of this part of the process.

Then comes the whittling. I suppose my natural inclination in 3-D work is to model, and whittling has that quality.

This stage is a delicate teasing out of the personality of the little person, perhaps a quality in its mouth or dimples in the cheeks. The person is in there and a gentle meditative approach seems to allow it to emerge. I enjoy this stage, it is mysterious and seems to

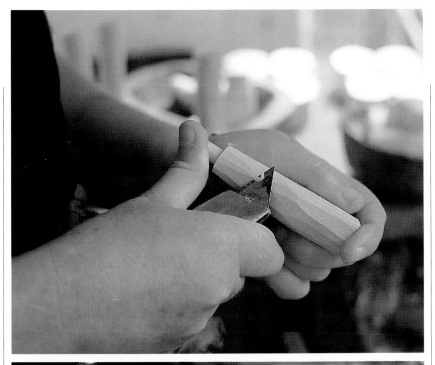

Top **The good old Stanley knife.**
Above **It is surprising how much character can be expressed in a boot.**

....

involve a bit of magic.

I have scoured catalogues for a better tool with which to whittle than my beloved Stanley knife, but the one I wrote off for doesn't keep its edge, and when I'm sitting by the Rayburn whittling away, I don't fancy going out to the cold workshop to sharpen it, when it is so easy to simply change the blade.

EXTREMITIES

Feet and hands require less concentration and I often work these at Covent Garden market where I have a regular fortnightly Sunday stall.

People watch in morbid fascination, a look of horror on their faces, waiting I suspect, not for the emergence of a perfect foot, but for fingers to fly! But as yet, I still have all eight, and two thumbs. I do usually wear a leather thumb-stall.

The sanding and painting need no comment, and assembly and dressing are also outside the woodcarver's domain.

There is no doubt that wood, for me, has a special magic. To use any other material for my dolls would have no appeal for me.

It is strong yet gentle, feels alive in my hands, seems to enjoy being metamorphosed, and has a wicked sense of humour.

When a blemish resembling a spot appears on the end of the nose of a face you have laboured over devotedly, or a shake suddenly manifests, what can you do but smile and acknowledge that you'll never be the master and that to work with wood is a privilege, not a right. ●

Auriel Mims completed her Diploma in Art & Design in painting at Chelsea School of Art in the mid 1960s. She worked at Bethnal Green Museum of Childhood as a museum assistant, where her interest in dolls began. She launched her Norfolk Dolls series three years ago.
She can be contacted at
Wayside Cottage, Thwaite Common, Erpingham, Norfolk NR11 7QQ
Tel: 01263 761665

GOING WITH THE GRAIN

DAVID CLARK DESCRIBES THE PROBLEMS HE ENCOUNTERED WHEN CARVING SOME FIGURES IN OLD, SPLIT YEW

There was an old yew (*Taxus baccata*) stump about 760mm, 30in high in front of my garden rubbish heap, and in the summer of 1993 I asked a friend with a chainsaw to cut it down.

It made six logs of dubious quality, because it was rotten in the middle. But I thought I might turn some small bowls or lidded boxes out of them.

In the autumn of the following year I took a two-month break. I left behind the possibility of woodturning, but discovered there was a woodcarver's studio in the grounds at The Abbey, Sutton Courtenay.

Teddy Hutton was the resident woodcarver, and I took with me a few gouges and a handy mallet, and one of the logs.

The only woodcarving I had done before was a linear gothic crucifix in pencil cedar (*Juniperus virginiana*) when I was 18, and two strange pieces three years before, a head in limewood (*Tilia Vulgaris*) and a small yew figure. I had no developed techniques.

I thought woodcarving would involve a lot of tedious chisel and mallet work getting rid of surplus wood before getting down to the serious business of fine carving.

At the Abbey studio I saw the carving potential of the Arbortech and the Powerfile with its continuous sanding belt, and realised that such tedium was a thing of the past.

But the yew log remained in my room, the object of long contemplation. What was in it? I looked at it every day for two weeks and the gentle curve of the tree impressed itself upon me.

After a while I decided to make a start and clear away the rotten wood to see what was left.

The Arbortech is a fierce tool and it took me a while to learn how to control it. Eventually it became a fairly accurate carving tool in my hands, digging out hollows and quickly removing surplus wood.

The curve of the sapwood began to suggest an angel's wings and there seemed to be enough solid wood on the left of the log for a kneeling woman's form.

I had noticed the teacher of a creative relaxation workshop I had attended kneeling in just this position. At the time I had sketched her quickly in charcoal. Now, I took up a pencil and sketchbook and made a few quick outlines of possibilities.

....

Original design sketches.

....

The raw block of yew. It contained rotten areas and splits, and a vein of purple.

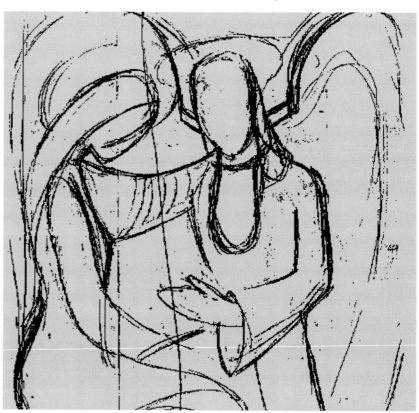

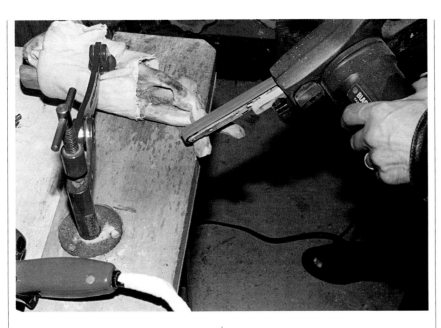

ANNUNCIATION

My next thought was this was big stuff. I could hardly attempt what was essentially an Annunciation theme with so little woodcarving experience. Surely, Tilman Riemenschneider did an apprenticeship and journeyman's work before tackling this sort of thing. But then another voice inside me said, risk it.

My excitement grew as the grain began to reveal itself. There was a vein of purple just inside the sapwood which was exposed as I chiselled out the shape of the wings at the back.

If I was careful this would colour the inside of the wings too, and the curling lines of the grain could suggest feathers.

With careful strokes of the chisel watching the grain all the time, I could play with those lines. And the dark closer grain suggested the fall of both the angel's and the woman's hair.

As I was cutting into the concave of the wing on the right side, tragedy struck. I knew there was a split, but hoped it would hold. Instead it widened.

Teddy Hutton, who was used to wood splitting, was undismayed. "Glue it", he said. So I poured ordinary

Using the Powerfile to shape a piece of yew root.

woodworker's adhesive into the crack and held it together with masking tape. With the other vertical marks in the wood, the split was virtually invisible.

Early last year, after displaying the piece in an exhibition, another split caused the wing to fall off. The same process proved effective.

PROPORTIONS

Another problem for me was proportion. The figures were taking shape nicely, but the woman's head was lumpish with its headcloth, and the angel's head was too big and square. I was terrified of taking off too much wood.

What should I do about noses and eyes and mouths? Yew splits notoriously easily. I had made the angel's face too flat for a proper nose and I considered the kneeling figure's face inaccessible.

I decided to risk being accused of copping out and to have the faces featureless, leaving more to the imagination and to the body language of the figures.

So I took up the Powerfile and removed the headcloth and was pleased with the simplicity of the result. Remember a face is always wedge-shaped, and I felt my own jaw to confirm it.

The belt sander brought about rapid transformation. I completed the angel's hairline, framing the face and his neckline with a small V-shaped gouge, taking care to sharpen it thoroughly first.

The angel's hip under his elbow remained a problem. There was too much of him. He must seem to have floated into the maiden's presence, and the lower part of his body must disappear.

Again my fear of taking off too much wood surfaced, but as I removed more and more, the pleasing inclination of the angel's body towards the maiden was emphasised and the wing looked lighter and more free.

Next I needed to dig out the space between the two figures. As I did so another stronger purple streak appeared in the grain under the

The finished figures in yew, 340mm, 13¼in high.

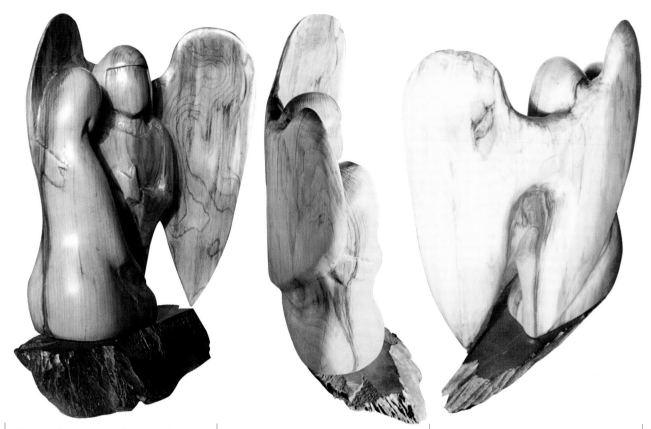

The purple streak can be seen down the back of the woman's figure and the split down the angel's wing.

The grain pattern was used to suggest feathers and hair. The purple streak can clearly be seen down the woman's back.

Rear of the figures, showing the grain pattern and splits in the wing.

left forearm of the angel. It delineated naturally a long loose sleeve, and needed only a little emphasis with the gouge at the opening.

When I dug out the stump six months later for more carving wood, I found a root crossing a rusty iron pipe which was drawing up the colour!

MESSAGE

Since this piece took so long in the making, what did it mean to me? It could be a fairly conventional Annunciation scene: the angel Gabriel bringing the message to Mary, "Fear not, Mary, for you have found favour with God. You shall conceive and bear a son, and you shall call him Jesus".

I also had other ideas: the guardian angel protecting, or comforting, the anima (soul), or simply a winged messenger bringing assurance of love to a young woman.

There was nothing in the carving to suggest this was the Annunciation, no Madonna lily beloved of medieval iconographers, no words engraved.

In an earlier sketch I had drawn a scroll and the incised lettering FEAR NOT across the lower body of the angel. In fact the interpretation sprang from my mind, built on past experience.

Finally, my break over, I brought the carving home. How should I finish it? I tried button polish at first and it produced a brilliant shine. Too much, I thought, and I sanded it off with fine sandpaper.

I next applied a little furniture polish and it took on the sort of matt shine I felt appropriate for the piece.

It looked rather squat on the level surface. Somehow it needed to be lifted on a contrasting material.

In the Leicestershire uplands there is a lot of slate lying about. So I selected a fine blue piece of the right thickness and took it down to my stonemason's yard, where they kindly ground flat the top and bottom of it.

I am a hoarder by nature and it took only a moment's foraging in my utility room to find a couple of old 100mm, 4in screws to fix the carving through the slate after drilling holes with a stonemason's drill.

Finally, I found this composition had slowly emerged from the wood itself. I felt I had gone with the grain in a deeper sense, and had a pleasing result which was good both to look at and to touch.

The finished angel and woman was 255 x 340mm high, 10 x 13¼in. ●

The Rev David Clark has been interested in the arts since childhood, but did not start carving until he was 18. He became a Church of England priest and was for 15 years industrial chaplain in Norwich. For the last 11 years he has been Team Rector in the parish of Oadby, Leicester. He is also a professional tenor. In the last eight years he has discovered woodturning and his mother-in-law's carving gouges.

INDEX

GMC Publications

WOODWORKING

40 More Woodworking Plans & Projects	GMC Publications	Making Chairs and Tables	GMC Publications
Bird Boxes and Feeders for the Garden	Dave Mackenzie	Making Fine Furniture	Tom Darby
Complete Woodfinishing	Ian Hosker	Making Little Boxes from Wood	John Bennett
Electric Woodwork	Jeremy Broun	Making Shaker Furniture	Barry Jackson
Furniture & Cabinetmaking Projects	GMC Publications	Pine Furniture Projects for the Home	Dave Mackenzie
Furniture Projects	Rod Wales	Sharpening Pocket Reference Book	Jim Kingshott
Furniture Restoration (Practical Crafts)	Kevin Jan Bonner	Sharpening: The Complete Guide	Jim Kingshott
Furniture Restoration and Repair for Beginners	Kevin Jan Bonner	Stickmaking: A Complete Course	Andrew Jones & Clive George
Green Woodwork	Mike Abbott	Woodfinishing Handbook (Practical Crafts)	Ian Hosker
The Incredible Router	Jeremy Broun	Woodworking Plans and Projects	GMC Publications
Making & Modifying Woodworking Tools	Jim Kingshott	The Workshop	Jim Kingshott

WOODTURNING

Adventures in Woodturning	David Springett	Practical Tips for Turners & Carvers	GMC Publications
Bert Marsh: Woodturner	Bert Marsh	Practical Tips for Woodturners	GMC Publications
Bill Jones' Notes from the Turning Shop	Bill Jones	Spindle Turning	GMC Publications
Bill Jones' Further Notes from the Turning Shop	Bill Jones	Turning Miniatures in Wood	John Sainsbury
Colouring Techniques for Woodturners	Jan Sanders	Turning Wooden Toys	Terry Lawrence
Decorative Techniques for Woodturners	Hilary Bowen	Understanding Woodturning	Ann & Bob Phillips
Essential Tips for Woodturners	GMC Publications	Useful Techniques for Woodturners	GMC Publications
Faceplate Turning	GMC Publications	Useful Woodturning Projects	GMC Publications
Fun at the Lathe	R.C. Bell	Woodturning: A Foundation Course	Keith Rowley
Illustrated Woodturning Techniques	John Hunnex	Woodturning: A Source Book of Shapes	John Hunnex
Intermediate Woodturning Projects	GMC Publications	Woodturning Jewellery	Hilary Bowen
Keith Rowley's Woodturning Projects	Keith Rowley	Woodturning Masterclass	Tony Boase
Make Money from Woodturning	Ann & Bob Phillips	Woodturning Techniques	GMC Publications
Multi-Centre Woodturning	Ray Hopper	Woodturning Test Reports	GMC Publications
Pleasure and Profit from Woodturning	Reg Sherwin	Woodturning Wizardry	David Springett

WOODCARVING

The Art of the Woodcarver	GMC Publications	Useful Techniques for Woodcarvers	GMC Publications
Carving Birds & Beasts	GMC Publications	Wildfowl Carving - Volume 1	Jim Pearce
Carving on Turning	Chris Pye	Wildfowl Carving - Volume 2	Jim Pearce
Carving Realistic Birds	David Tippey	The Woodcarvers	GMC Publications
Decorative Woodcarving	Jeremy Williams	Woodcarving: A Complete Course	Ron Butterfield
Essential Tips for Woodcarvers	GMC Publications	Woodcarving: A Foundation Course	Zoë Gertner
Essential Woodcarving Techniques	Dick Onians	Woodcarving for Beginners	GMC Publications
Lettercarving in Wood: A Practical Course	Chris Pye	Woodcarving Test Reports	GMC Publications
Practical Tips for Turners & Carvers	GMC Publications	Woodcarving Tools, Materials & Equipment	Chris Pye
Understanding Woodcarving	GMC Publications		

UPHOLSTERY

Seat Weaving (Practical Crafts)	Ricky Holdstock	Upholstery Restoration	David James
Upholsterer's Pocket Reference Book	David James	Upholstery Techniques & Projects	David James
Upholstery: A Complete Course	David James		

TOYMAKING

Designing & Making Wooden Toys	Terry Kelly	Making Wooden Toys & Games	Jeff & Jennie Loader
Fun to Make Wooden Toys & Games	Jeff & Jennie Loader	Restoring Rocking Horses	Clive Green & Anthony Dew
Making Board, Peg & Dice Games	Jeff & Jennie Loader		

DOLLS' HOUSES

Architecture for Dolls' Houses	*Joyce Percival*	Making Miniature Oriental Rugs & Carpets	*Meik & Ian McNaughton*
Beginners' Guide to the Dolls' House Hobby	*Jean Nisbett*	Making Period Dolls' House Accessories	*Andrea Barham*
The Complete Dolls' House Book	*Jean Nisbett*	Making Period Dolls' House Furniture	*Derek & Sheila Rowbottom*
Dolls' House Bathrooms: Lots of Little Loos	*Patricia King*	Making Tudor Dolls' Houses	*Derek Rowbottom*
Easy to Make Dolls' House Accessories	*Andrea Barham*	Making Unusual Miniatures	*Graham Spalding*
Make Your Own Dolls' House Furniture	*Maurice Harper*	Making Victorian Dolls' House Furniture	*Patricia King*
Making Dolls' House Furniture	*Patricia King*	Miniature Needlepoint Carpets	*Janet Granger*
Making Georgian Dolls' Houses	*Derek Rowbottom*	The Secrets of the Dolls' House Makers	*Jean Nisbett*

CRAFTS

Celtic Knotwork Designs	*Sheila Sturrock*	Making Greetings Cards for Beginners	*Pat Sutherland*
Collage from Seeds, Leaves and Flowers	*Joan Carver*	Making Knitwear Fit	*Pat Ashforth & Steve Plummer*
Complete Pyrography	*Stephen Poole*	Needlepoint: A Foundation Course	*Sandra Hardy*
Creating Knitwear Designs	*Pat Ashforth & Steve Plummer*	Pyrography Handbook (Practical Crafts)	*Stephen Poole*
Cross Stitch Kitchen Projects	*Janet Granger*	Tassel Making for Beginners	*Enid Taylor*
Cross Stitch on Colour	*Sheena Rogers*	Tatting Collage	*Lindsay Rogers*
Embroidery Tips & Hints	*Harold Hayes*	Temari: A Traditional Japanese	
An Introduction to Crewel Embroidery	*Mave Glenny*	Embroidery Technique	*Margaret Ludlow*
Making Character Bears	*Valerie Tyler*		

THE HOME

Home Ownership: Buying and Maintaining	*Nicholas Snelling*	Security for the Householder:	
		Fitting Locks and Other Devices	*E. Phillips*

VIDEOS

Drop-in and Pinstuffed Seats	*David James*	Twists and Advanced Turning	*Dennis White*
Stuffover Upholstery	*David James*	Sharpening the Professional Way	*Jim Kingshott*
Elliptical Turning	*David Springett*	Sharpening Turning & Carving Tools	*Jim Kingshott*
Woodturning Wizardry	*David Springett*	Bowl Turning	*John Jordan*
Turning Between Centres: The Basics	*Dennis White*	Hollow Turning	*John Jordan*
Turning Bowls	*Dennis White*	Woodturning: A Foundation Course	*Keith Rowley*
Boxes, Goblets and Screw Threads	*Dennis White*	Carving a Figure: The Female Form	*Ray Gonzalez*
Novelties and Projects	*Dennis White*	The Router: A Beginner's Guide	*Alan Goodsell*
Classic Profiles	*Dennis White*	The Scroll Saw: A Beginner's Guide	*John Burke*

MAGAZINES

WOODTURNING ◆ WOODCARVING ◆ TOYMAKING

FURNITURE & CABINETMAKING ◆ BUSINESSMATTERS

CREATIVE IDEAS FOR THE HOME ◆ THE ROUTER

———————— ◆ ————————

The above represents a full list of all titles currently published or scheduled to be published. All are available direct from the Publishers or through bookshops, newsagents and specialist retailers. To place an order, or to obtain a complete catalogue, contact:

GMC Publications,
166 High Street, Lewes, East Sussex BN7 1XU, United Kingdom
Tel: 01273 488005 Fax: 01273 478606

Orders by credit card are accepted